Life Reco

Life Reconnected

How Women Can Make Simple and Powerful Change

A Hero's Journey

Penny C McClean

Matador
9 Priory Business Park,
Wistow Road, Kibworth Beauchamp,
Leicestershire. LE8 0RX
Tel: (+44) 116 279 2299
Fax: (+44) 116 279 2277
Email: books@troubador.co.uk
Web: www.troubador.co.uk/matador

ISBN 978 1780885 100

British Library Cataloguing in Publication Data.
A catalogue record for this book is available from the British Library.

Typeset in 11pt Georgia by Troubador Publishing Ltd, Leicester, UK

Matador is an imprint of Troubador Publishing Ltd

For A, R and J.

"The real point of being alive is to evolve into the whole person you were intended to be"

Oprah Winfrey

"Many women today feel a sadness we cannot name. Though we accomplish much of what we set out to do, we sense that something is missing in our lives and – fruitlessly – search 'out there' for the answers. What's often wrong is that we are disconnected from an authentic sense of self"

Emily Hancock, Author of *The Girl Within*

"How does one describe, not one's circumstances or what one did at any particular time of one's life, but what one was?"

Gitta Sereny, Journalist and Author

"Our intuition can scare us silly. It often goes against what we think is the safe option. It is a constant, always guiding us, but often we don't like what it is telling us...

...It was such a powerful feeling, a 'get real' moment, that all fear dropped away. I realised that never again could I take the safe road and ignore the intuition that guided me. I saw that life, lived fully, had no guarantees, only experiences that constantly taught me to grow, push the comfort-zone boundary and live life to the fullest"

Jessica McGregor Johnson,
Author of *Remembering Perfection*

Contents

FOREWORD

One Potato, Two Potato…

"She's just like a man!" my mother snarls as Martina Navratilova whips a forehand cross court winner past the beautiful but stretched legs of Chris Evert.

"Hmmn. More tea?" I reply.

Clearly seeing too many balls on court, (Specsavers still had a way to go) as down the years at mealtimes too my mother presented another pair of balls in the shape of the two potatoes that she regularly dished up to the men in my family without question. "Do you want another potato, Penny?" she would ask me, as she surreptitiously plonked another one on her own plate.

"No thanks, one's enough," I'd reply without conviction.

By 1982 I had bought the book A Woman In Your Own Right by Anne Dickson. I knew she was right and that women needed to be more assertive in their lives. Later I began teaching assertiveness skills myself mostly to groups of young women and most of them young mothers. I was passionate in helping these young women see that they were in fact doing one of the most important jobs in the world (parenting) and that they were the most important role model in their child's life. For some of them it was the first time they had ever been told they were good at something or that they were important in any way.

As my professional career in supporting women continued I used to say that at some stage in every woman's life she would encounter something that revealed to her an unfairness due to her gender. For me I faced it square on in childbirth when being told to give birth in a position that served the view of the physicians, most of them male, rather than the natural and most optimal one for any mother and child. The view they face (in this case my birthing canal) had always been deemed more important and dictated the development of an entire system of delivering babies with women lying on their backs. That system had gone unchallenged for years.

For other women it is in their jobs, in sport, in their roles within families or relationships, or their own encounter with a professional system or whatever. For more yet it is just in an observation about popular culture generally or political leadership specifically and for several more years after reading the book I continued with my own observations as Anne D would say, 'passively'. And I was bored with it.

Fast forward to today and the world has changed dramatically since Martina dominated the women's tennis game and I bought that book. The digital age has brought us freedoms unimaginable just a few years ago and women the world over have more access to personal independence than ever before. Unless you live in parts of Africa, Asia and many other places too.

Here in the West though, and particularly at latitude 54 degrees N and almost 6 degrees W, some things just stay the same. I know that attitudinal change is slow. I understand the difference between attitude change and corresponding behaviour change. In other words I know there is a time gap. I also know the importance of positive role models that each and every one of us takes messages from, even if we don't realise it.

And I still hear women saying they can't do certain things – they're not confident enough, they're not knowledgeable enough and they are definitely not thin enough as they go about their lives unwittingly promoting men and their stories of leadership, science, progression, influence and importance. We're all doing it most of the time and it's not actually that difficult to understand why.

When I hit a crisis point in my life I had to stop and reflect on many things. My own years of conditioning about how women could and should be in the world had been challenged many times up to that point. I was thought of as being a 'strong' woman, fairly confident and all of those 'teach what you need to learn' assertiveness classes had gone some way to push against what I call the 'thin web' that surrounds what women are trying to achieve in their lives. Sometimes you poke little holes and break through the web, but you are somehow still attached and it sticks to you in bits until you really shake it off.

I went on a profound personal journey and here's what I found on the way. Hold the front page – we are different from men. There's more – we are constantly being fed what is good for men, not what is good for women. By being fed I don't mean the extra potatoes, I mean the food of our brains in the messages we get, the stories that are promoted, the role models from all of history, what we see and hear on TV and radio, what politicians decide for us, what business leaders, managers and trainers tell us, what authors promote as self-help for women and the biggest one of all – what we say to each other as women. I've been as guilty as anyone. We are all conditioned, still.

This book is for you if you are a young woman who is just beginning your journey into adulthood and your life of career, relationships, family and your contribution to the world. It is also for any woman who is a leader, trainer, teacher, mentor, parent, entrepreneur, business owner, politician or youth worker. Anyone who has the ability to influence and empower our young women leaders of the future. It will take you on a profound personal journey. In so doing together we can acknowledge, celebrate and become inspired by the lives of other women that already make up this big society we live in and in turn become inspired by our own intuitive wisdom and knowledge. We can find our own unique voice and we can start a new conversation, one that moves women forward.

...Three Potato, Four

Life Reconnected is about capacity building in women. It offers a new and tailor-made process for women to reconnect with what is important in their lives and a new network of women that builds for the future, reflects on the inspiration of others and allows us to live fully empowered in the present. It presents and illustrates through one woman's story the psychological models that make the most of difference. What it is that can empower, inspire and reconnect us with what is really meaningful in our lives as we move forward in this century. Just four principles can do it.

We'll be using a model of change that explains how the pain of confusion is actually beneficial and necessary; discovering how we use language and scripting, and finding out that how we have been taught and reinforced to see ourselves all matters, and can help us. This book describes how we can use this to incorporate the four key principles of Balance, Connectedness, Love and Purpose to have a life we not only love to live but one that doesn't fear change. Rather, change is seen as the necessary part of a life well lived.

We can't change the facts of our lives but we can change the story. Story changes perspective and that can change your feelings about the facts. How we voice that story and how we tell it to ourselves and others is the difference that makes the difference. It is powerful and Anne D was right in 1982 and she is right in 2012, it can change your life.

And if all that's too boring for you try this for size.

You're a woman and you are powerful, resourceful and have an amazing ability to make brilliant decisions that affect your life and the lives of your loved ones around you. It's time to step up. You just need to give yourself a shake – and here it is...

PART I

Does My Brain Look Big In This?

CHAPTER ONE

No, Not *Another* Diet for Women, Just New Brain Food

As women we need to move through change many times in our lives. Sometimes it's easy, sometimes we're not so surefooted – we need *tailored* support that we haven't had before.

"I can't believe this is happening again."

"It's not the same."

"It is. I've been here before and I can't cope with this again."

"Although some of it may feel the same, you have never actually been here before. It is different. You have never been on this particular square on the board of life before."

She was right. I hadn't been there before even though it felt like I had made the biggest mistake of my life. Again.

"Get up off your knees and look around the green field that is your life," she went on.

Instead of seeing the green field, I was gazing on a life that had unravelled in front of me and all that was left was loss. My father had just died after a very sudden and intensive period of ill health, my partner had also left my life and somewhere along the way I had also shed both my home and my job. My health was not great and to top it all I had reached that dreaded stage in life that could no longer be denied – midlife. I had grief, loss, regret, depression and an utter, utter sense of pointlessness stacking in my mind above my now twisting, hurting body. The biggest loss of all was my own sense of self. I didn't know who I was anymore.

Change

Change. It is an inevitable part of life. We are born, we develop, we decline and we die. There are psychological developmental models of it – stages of our cognitive development, childhood, adolescence, adulthood and old age. There are biological models of it, psychosocial models and we live *in* a world that is constantly changing too from the cycles of day and night, the yearly turn of the earth around the sun to the very fact of our universe expanding all the time. Heck, here in Northern Ireland we can have all four seasons in the space of an afternoon.

Nature is continuously flagging up to us the circle and cycle of life. Sometimes we can take comfort in it and sometimes we want to cling on to something as if the very purpose of our life depends on keeping it the same.

As women that cycle of life is rarely far from our minds as our bodies are functioning in their own rhythms of renewal and repeat for most of our post-puberty lives. Women's lives also have their own rhythms as we move through them, sometimes with multiple roles as carers, partners, home makers, mothers, daughters, business owners etc. We have taken on those roles and we love our partners, children, families, homes and businesses to bits. Sometimes we come unstuck and find that is exactly what we have – bits of ourselves that don't seem to make up a complete whole any more. Sound at all familiar?

Much has been written, researched and spoken about women and 'the change' and it certainly is a developmental stage that can bring about a whole new way of being in the world. A new crisis point has also been identified as the quarter-life crisis to rack up alongside the traditional midlife one as twentysomethings find they need to take stock of what they are doing with their lives.

But change can also come, not in some ordered or prescribed developmental stage, but sometimes like what one woman described to me as:

"*...an absolute curve ball that came out of the blue. Nothing smooth or predictable about it at all but a very effective wake-up call nonetheless which ultimately led to some very fulfilling changes for me.*"

Maybe even more of us are in bits than we realise. Do you feel your life is out of whack in some way? Going through a loss, heartbreak or some big change that is a bit overwhelming for you? If so Life Reconnected is for you. I'm going to stretch your thinking until you get a new perspective on whatever your own personal situation may be and you find you can make meaningful change and have a life you love to live.

Role Models

After years of working with women I've heard the same thing over and over again about our lack of knowledge, confidence, finances or whatever. I see women hesitate when the opportunity to step up into a leadership role presents itself especially if they can move aside and let their male peers do so instead. We're also constantly seeking permission to do different things in our lives and to be different from the roles we have been assigned because of our gender.

So why are we so lacking in confidence and happy to put others on the grand stage that is life? I believe that at least part of it is because we haven't had empowering messages about how successful we are as women, nor have we heard and seen enough strong female leaders and thinkers and so we lose a sense of who *we* really can be, who *we* as women really are.

I've watched trainers in Belfast and London, in the corporate sector and in the not-for-profit, in business training, in equality and diversity training, and both female and male trainers use examples of theories, illustrations of points of discussion, clips from movies and stories of science and progress that are almost to a fault examples of men doing all these things. All these examples are being promoted as positive behaviours for both men and women. It *can't not* be having an effect.

It Is Different For Women. We Are Different AND We Can Make The Most Of That Difference.

We have had a different set of messages and fewer role models to learn from and we generally have been brought up differently from our brothers within our own families, and to other men in our peer groups. This is not a political statement on equality but an observation that if we receive different signals and messages we are going to make different meaning in our brains.

Our biology is also different and our hormonal drives do play a part on the different states our brains may be in. This in turn affects how we see ourselves with all the attendant limitations and beliefs that affect how we behave.

Then, when we women hit a crisis or period of great change in our lives we feel ill-equipped to deal with it, are overly critical of our achievement and compare ourselves to what is perceived as the norm which is generally not a reflection of the reality of women's lives.

Most of the psychological models of helping people understand and move through change are written, researched and published/promoted by men. That's great but we as women do think differently and generally do have different lives and actually there are brilliant women transformational leaders out there using their own intuitive wisdom and experience. It just shouldn't be the case that if you haven't read one or two particular books or heard one or two inspirational women speak you miss the positive influence. It can be all around us and we can hear it all the time if we look, listen and speak in a different direction.

We can also make the most of our difference. We can understand how we construct the story of our lives with the backdrop of messages we receive and we can make changes brilliantly by using that difference to our advantage.

They Are There

Even in 2012 there are few women leaders, policy makers, business owners, recognised thinkers and scientists – or are there? Maybe we just haven't been given the role models or their stories, as popular culture tends to be driven by male decision-makers in journalism, the media etc.

Just this morning on the BBC, Winter Olympic gold medal-winner Amy Williams was being interviewed about her retirement from sport and the interviewer mentioned that a news piece that day was about introducing different games into PE in schools to encourage more girls to take part in sports. The interviewer asked Amy if she thought this was a good idea and Amy replied that we needed more positive role models of women in sport and then struggled to think quickly of more than one or two. I struggled too.

Coverage of male sport on television is an obvious and easy target of making my point but it does go some way to illustrate how these things are important. (NB the BBC are now making a huge effort to redress their own biased reporting of sport in the light of the BBC Sports Personality of the Year debacle last year (2011) when not one female sports person was shortlisted. They also recently lost an unfair dismissal case brought against them by a woman presenter who had ultimately been replaced by a younger female presenter while her aging male counterparts remained gainfully employed).

We struggle to think of female sporting icons because we rarely see or hear of them in the mainstream media and clearly I am not the only person making the connection between having positive role models and the uptake and success of female sporting stars (take a bow swimmer Rebecca Adlington, and Maggie Alphonsi, the iconic woman's rugby player who was voted the Sunday Times Sportswoman of the Year. And Amy Williams too). Do you know what sport Amy Williams won her Olympic gold medal for? (Hint: it involves hurtling yourself down a frozen track face down on nothing much more than a board with neither a steering nor braking mechanism!)

The 2012 Olympics have been called the Women's Olympics as there are not only many female hopeful medal winners, but they have been involved at every level in making the games happen. In a recent interview for the magazine Good Housekeeping, Clare Balding, one of the BBC presenting team, said, *"I really hope that the Olympics change the perception of women's sport. In non-Olympic years, you get almost no women's sports being covered, so you end up with an all-male shortlist for BBC Sports Personality of the Year like last year – because nobody knows what women have done! In the next 10 years I want to change the world, and the way I want to do it is to make sure, however I can, that there is more basic coverage of women's sport... And I think any girl under the age of 17 watching the Games will get so much more of a positive outlook on body shape. It shows what a healthy, fit woman's body looks like – and it's not a size zero."*

In the same article Baroness Tanni Grey-Thompson, a Paralympian with an astonishing 11 gold medals and who is deeply committed to improving women's involvement and diversity in sport said, "*Women were sidelined in British sport for a long time, and it wasn't until 1984 that women were allowed to run the marathon! But although things are getting better, there's still a long way to go. We need to get more women on boards, because that's how things will change. Sports are recognising now that they need to run like businesses and be more diverse. I'm on the diversity board of the London Organising Committee of the Olympic and Paralympic Games (LOCOG), and half of LOCOG's management team is female, which is a pretty good place to be. We're getting there!*"

Even the Olympics Aquatics Centre was designed by the Iraqi-British architect Zaha Hadid. She became the first woman to win the Pritzker Architecture prize, the equivalent of a Nobel Prize in her field.

As women we need to stop holding back and putting ourselves down. We can challenge ourselves and stretch our own thinking. We can look and find positive female role models to help us. They are there.

Thinking Space

It is also important to give women a new space to reconnect with what is really important in their lives. A space that is not about excluding men. That is about encouraging and connecting as women to give support to the particular needs in a woman's life.

Virginia Woolf wrote in 1928 that 'a woman must have money and a room of one's own' to write fiction. I am writing now that what we need is a space of our own – thinking space of our own – to achieve a balance and connection in our lives. When women have that then everyone wins because only when we connect with our authentic selves do we go on to make informed choices and make meaningful relationships with both women and men.

Years of conditioning about how we as women 'should' be in the world haven't really helped. But we *can* change how we feel by changing how we feed and use our brains – i.e. how we think and how we talk. Firstly to ourselves and secondly how we speak out into the world – it's about understanding our psychology and making conversations that move women forward. It's about finding your own unique voice and letting it be heard.

We receive mixed messages all the time about how the world is for women, including subliminal messages we are not consciously aware of and even messages from those who are trying to help women achieve more in their lives – because of the examples and stories they use. They can reinforce the stereotype that those who really 'know' things are not women. That on the whole the examples we need to follow are not of women.

A Little Bit Of Psychology

You may have heard of Neuro Linguistic Programming (NLP). At its most basic description it is a psychological model of how we take in, process and make sense of information to in turn make sense of our lives. What I especially love about it is that it is more *process* than content-oriented. The distinction between these two lies at the heart of most NLP work. As an illustration of this: a traditional therapist working with a client might get the person to relive various unpleasant experiences from their past with a lot of detail – what she said, I said and what I did etc to try to diminish the power of these memories, i.e. it is detailed and *content* focused.

An NLP practitioner is more interested in how people have programmed and use these memories now, and, if the result is limiting or damaging to the person, in breaking the pattern of current use. Do you think it would be useful to identify any unhelpful programmes we might be running? I do. Do you think it would be useful to have some new tools to change the programme if you choose to do so? Again I think so. While the content may on some level be more interesting, it may be a distraction from what is really going on in a person with a particular thought pattern.

Just Four Principles

And so NLP models can give us a set of tools to help make those changes and in this book I'm going to take you on a process that uses some of those tools to particularly help you as a woman.

Life Reconnected believes that you are naturally creative and completely capable of finding your own answers to whatever change or challenge you face and it offers a framework and toolkit to facilitate this. I'm going to present four principles which, if you can incorporate them, you will have a life you love to live whether you are a twenty or thirtysomething and just out into the mad, mad world or in midlife and reflecting on what has passed, or what is yet to come. There is the life you've planned – and there's always what comes next!

We can hear and see *new* messages, it's never too late to change.

We can tell a different story. Now let's begin...

CHAPTER TWO

It's OK Not To Be OK

Change is inevitable. It is sure to happen. You haven't done anything wrong or bad or stupid. If something isn't working in your life it is simply because you haven't got the tools or techniques to access all that you really need to put it right. As Maya Angelou said, "when we know better, we do better." You actually already have all that you need, you just don't know it yet and that too is ok, you will know soon. Change is inevitable but personal growth is actually a choice…

Forget the could have, would have, should have. Sometimes life is hard and messy and painful and we're not really perfect are we? Or, maybe we are perfect but life is sometimes hard and messy and painful. What if that really was it and we actually are perfect?

Sit for a moment and close your eyes and think about yourself and your life and how it would be if you believed, really believed, you were perfect. Imagine you had grown up always being told you were important and clever and could do anything you put your mind to. Not only were you told this but you noticed it too in how people behaved around you. You felt that you were so important people would look to you for instruction, would listen to your opinions and that when you spoke, people would listen and they would take care of your needs. See yourself moving through life knowing and feeling and experiencing that.

Did it feel any different?

Now let's look at how you are telling this story of what is wrong in your life. Falling apart? What are you telling yourself, exactly? Write down, right now, what is wrong in your life. Do any of these cover it – I'm confused, I've done it again, I feel guilty, I'm bored, my life is crap, I'm not confident enough, nothing ever works out for me, if they only knew, how come they get all the credit?, he left me, she left me, I don't know enough, I do know enough but nobody listens to me, I'm all alone, is this it?, they don't really love me, where's the bally dog? Okay that last one is a little trite but you get my drift. Keep that little life statement for the next chapter, we'll find your dog.

Confusion Is Good. Welcome It.

If you weren't confused or scared or even overwhelmed and in pain it would mean nothing of much significance was going to change and if you are reading this book you want something to change so that's a great starting point. For those of you just browsing, browse on...

This will move you forward – you either step forward into a new place of growth or remain stuck in a false safety. Or even worse, have a feeling of going backwards. Remember I thought I had 'done it again'? Well it was only what I was telling myself. We are never living exactly the same thing again and that gives us choice and an opportunity to change no matter how difficult our situation feels right now or what age or stage in life we are at.

Confusion signifies a period of growth, birth or rebirth, or a step into a new stage of life – think of all those transition stages we go through. Remember being a teenager and being all over the place as you tried to figure out who you were? Better yet remember trying to learn to tie your shoelaces or ride a bike? We can make many attempts, feel frustrated, humiliated, confused and then with time we get there and it seems on reflection like a doddle. It will be the same with you whatever transition you are going through now even if it's your career choices, relationships, health or even the very purpose of your life. In fact *especially* if it's the very purpose of your life. If you take this confusion, stretch your thinking and reconnect with what's important you'll see how it's ok not to feel ok.

Change, Again.

As described in Chapter One, change is integral to life. Psychological models of how we move through change have adapted over the years from those of a linear construct (i.e. that life is a continuum in a straight line of clearly defined stages including childhood, adolescence, adulthood and old age) with a particular outlook or view of the world that pertains to these developmental stages.

That model has been somewhat replaced by others that describe life as moving in a circle of continuous cycles. Here change applies to the whole life cycle including chapters (periods of stability) and transitions (when we are thrown off course in some way). Each of these chapters has clearly defined stages and we keep cycling through them as we move on in our years.

My favourite model is called Change House and here confusion even gets a room of its own. It describes life as a four-room dwelling to explain the cycle of change and the importance of confusion as we move from room to room throughout the house and ultimately our life cycle, buffeted by the winds of change. Anything that can take two of my past obsessions, namely confusion and houses, and make an imitation of life has got my attention already.

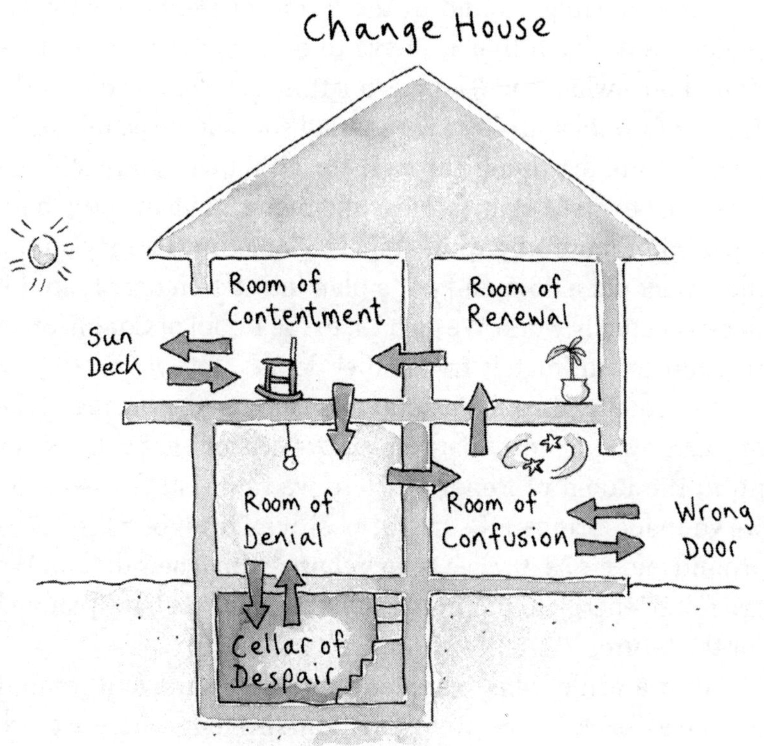

Change House was originally created by Claes Janssen. This illustration is by Bill Piggins, taken from Brilliant Decision Making by Robbie Steinhouse and reproduced here with kind permission from Pearson.

When life is trucking along nicely we are mostly in the Room of Contentment, even taking time to lie out on our sun deck enjoying the stability. The ebb and flow of life continues and ultimately things change and problems can emerge or something comes to an end. Gradually as things continue we move into the Room of Denial where everything kinda looks the same, but yet it feels different. Things may have gone wrong but we are pretending everything is still fine. As things get worse we may even sink into the Cellar of Despair.

After hanging around in the Room of Denial, finally we make the decision that we have to do something even if we don't know what it is. There is a letting go. We move into the Room of Confusion. Here we have all sorts of ideas, talking to people, thinking things through etc, although we are still not sure what to do. We can feel loss and regret, guilt and even have a period of mourning while in here. Sometimes we try out an idea, walk out a door and put a plan into action only to find it doesn't actually work. We go back to the Room of Confusion to regroup and ultimately try another door.

Eventually, through exploration and maybe through trial and error we will formulate a plan or decision that will take us up to the Room of Renewal. Here we find that the decision we've made brings all sorts of positive ideas, our life turns around and it's as if we've been 'reborn' with a new dream. We are full of energy to put in place the changes we have planned for the future.

After a while this excitement begins to wane and we find ourselves back in the Room of Contentment where we are enjoying the life we have made. Soon the sun deck beckons...

Confusion

Confusion can be a very scary state to be in. Sometimes it's as if everything we once knew to be true no longer makes sense anymore. For many women, who have spent their lives making their relationships and families the centre pin of their lives, change in the form of a relationship breaking down or ending, divorce, children leaving the nest or a bereavement can all throw us off course with such velocity that we no longer recognise ourselves anymore never mind our lives. For a lot of other women too, a successful career can begin to feel like a guilty pleasure when societal pressures to be the childbearer, nurturer and the homemaker rename us as that 'career woman' or, God forbid, 'just like a man'.

Others find that the Room of Denial can begin to seem safer and easier than making an attempt at changing something even in a situation where their very safety can be at risk. We deny our true feelings, we want things to stop or change but we feel powerless to create any real or meaningful change we can sustain. And for those who linger too long in here the descent into the Cellar of Despair is all too close.

Depression, that old companion for far too many women, can take root here, fueled by a tendency to ruminate and not let new beliefs temper our negative default thinking. We filter information that might help us and I'll talk more about filters and how our brains have to do this in the next chapter.

My own confusion whilst moving through a period of overwhelming change began to feel like my mind was stuck on a spin cycle that I could neither stop nor move on through to the next stage of my life's program. I was moving house again for the fifth time in two years (not good numbers) and the mantra I kept repeating to myself was "house, job, life; house, job, life," believing that if I could just buy a house then I could get a job and then I would have a life. Unfortunately for me the wash cycle before that spin could even begin ran something like "If I bought a house I would feel better about myself. If I felt better about myself I could buy a house." Round and round the thinking would go.

No one could understand (least of all me) why I couldn't "just buy any house!" Confusion reigned and I could feel that pull down into the Cellar of Despair as I seemed incapable of moving in any direction.

The truth was I was more in a state (or room) of denial and had not even got as far as the confusion stage. It was really only when I finally let go of the life I was trying desperately to hold on to and began with where I actually was, and what I actually had, that I was able to move forward.

Getting to acceptance rather than resignation and just *being* whatever we are in any one time is a powerful agent of change. We all know that what we resist persists and as Sally Brampton discovered and described in Shoot The Damn Dog, her memoir of depression:

"If there is any lesson I have learned from depression, it is this. We have to let go – of self-pity, anger and blame. We are what we are. Life is what it is. It will be what it is, however we are, and the best way to deal with it is gently. It took me a long time to learn that. In every psychiatric hospital all the psychiatrists, therapists and nurses kept saying the same thing. 'You must let go, Sally.' The trouble was, I did not understand what they meant and nor could they tell me how to do it. Whenever my mind wrapped in coils so black and tight and knotted that I thought they could never be undone, I tried to do as they suggested. The harder I tried, the more my mind seemed to hold on. And then I came across the writings of a Buddhist teacher... 'Letting go is not getting rid of. Letting go is letting be.' When I read that I felt one of those rare moments of clear, lucid understanding. It was a moment of light. Years of clenched meaningless slipped into place. The coils loosened and fell away. It did not last, of course. Nothing does. But it gave me a sufficient understanding to know that when I get into difficulty, the best way for me is not to try to let go, but to let it be."

Where are you in the cycle of change? Are you stuck on a spin cycle? Let's examine what to do when your life sucks and we begin with what actually is...

CHAPTER THREE

You Are Not Your Story!

> "When Mr and Mrs Dursley woke up on the dull, grey Tuesday our story starts, there was nothing about the cloudy sky outside to suggest that strange and mysterious things would soon be happening all over the country."
>
> From *Harry Potter and The Philosopher's Stone* by JK Rowling

Oh but I just love JK Rowling. Not only the fantastic stories she writes but the story of her, the author. About how she overcame a period of difficulty in her life, the loss she felt for her mother, the rejection slips, the fact that she was a single mother and felt she had made a bit of a mess of her life and then went on to write one of the most successful and brilliant publishing phenomena the world has ever seen. The fact that on tracing her family roots she recognised and gave credit to the strength of her female predecessors some of whom too had been single parents.

One Christmas a number of years ago I watched a documentary about her life and it was the most inspirational piece of television viewing I had seen for years. It was very moving to watch her revisit the flat where she had written the first Harry Potter book. She remarked that she would never have believed then that all these years later she would visit and see a copy of her published book on someone else's bookshelf.

Of course I don't know her personally but of what we have been able to see of her life I give thanks to the massively positive role model she is. Somewhere inside, JK Rowling knew she had a story to tell.

In her essay Whoever Tells The Best Story Wins: The Subjective Side of Business, Annette Simmons talks about the importance of telling a story to improve collaborative decision making and about how it can shift perspective. "Story is a reconstituted reality that awakens all the senses and conjures enough emotional glue for an idea to stick."

That's just it, ideas in stories do stick like a post-it note across our minds. Stories undoubtedly help us connect as human beings as they illustrate and access something innate. Like Annette Simmons says when we share stories that reveal our humanity, we connect at the level of human experience – the messy, confusing, emotional reality of real people living real lives.

This is why it is so critical to look at the story we tell ourselves, about ourselves. What is your story and how do you tell it? What are you saying about your capabilities or your skills? Is it your story or did someone else give it to you? The idea of it will stick and have an impact on how you feel about yourself and ultimately how you go about your life.

I'd like to tell you three stories. The first one is about a woman, let's call her Jane, and her story is called Plain Jane.

Jane was the youngest child of a family of four. A talkative skinny child who seemed to be forever playing catch up intellectually to the others in her family and who grew up thinking she was particularly ugly as she had been forever told she had a big nose and that if she stood sideways she would disappear.

She was also constantly being told to stop talking by her parents and teachers. Jane was very close to her mother, who constantly berated herself for being 'stupid' and who acted as a kind of buffer for her husband's intellectual sarcasm and his children's enquiring minds.

Jane grew up in a country that had huge political unrest and civil conflict that was at its height when she reached adolescence. Her teenage rebellion manifested itself in complete rejection of the political views of her parents, particularly of her father, and so she finally did stop talking to them both about anything of particular consequence.

Jane went on to marry a man of a very different political persuasion to her family, raised a family of her own and continued to live her life feeling she wasn't always able to speak and be heard about things that really mattered. She had a strong sense though that there was still something unfair about the society she lived in and that there was something that wasn't being said.

Prone to depression on and off throughout her married life, Jane's happiest times were those she shared simply and plainly with her young children. Basking in the complete fulfillment of motherhood it was a job she felt she really knew how to do and actually felt very supported by both of her own parents during this time.

Now let's meet Susan. Her story is called Science and Progress.

Susan had been a very active child with a keen skill in observing what was going on around her and in her family. She questioned everything that was given to her as absolutes and grew up with an interest in science, nature and the sheer wonder of the universe. She wanted to know how everything worked.

After leaving school she went to work in forensic science, involved in cutting-edge methods of detecting minute traces of explosives and firearm residue and she absolutely loved it. Her career in science continued, she married and when she became pregnant was as interested in the process of childbirth as any other scientific enquiry she made.

When she had her first child her interests developed

around human psychology and she returned to full-time study. Her social conscience had been awakened and she absolutely loved the science base to the human condition that psychology gave her. She was very interested in developmental psychology and in particular the development of self-esteem and parenting styles in relation to that development.

Susan's career developed into supporting people who were marginalised from society, helping them to feel more confident about making informed choices in their lives using the psychology she had studied as a basis for her work.

Finally let's meet Chris. Her story is called Is Chris Really A Lesbian?

Unlike Jane and Susan, Chris had been fearless as a child. Always keen to keep up with the boys and the older girls, Chris took part in all the games going, not letting anyone stop her if she could help it. She climbed trees, rode horses and felt physically very strong. Like Jane and Susan though she loved all the outdoor pursuits her family did and especially loved the outdoor camping and boating her dad was particularly interested in.

She was seen as quite a tough adolescent, always questioning authority, although she was quite funny and had a developing sensitivity to other people's feelings. Chris formed a few but very meaningful friendships throughout her teenage years, feeling she didn't really get what most of the other girls were interested in.

Chris then went on to work in local government, a chance job opportunity suggested by her father which led to a long and fulfilled career which took many turns as her life progressed.

On reaching middle age Chris hit a crisis in her life. Something that her physical strength, humour and life experience to that point couldn't help. She had been plagued by ill health for a number of years and had lost confidence in her body in a way she had never felt before. Her father had just died, her relationship with a woman who had been a source of strength in her life for over 13 years had broken down and after a series of decisions about her career was without a job for no reason she could sufficiently explain for the first time in her life. She had even sold her house at a time of emotional upheaval and was now feeling a complete or 'divine' homesickness. Her life felt meaningless, pointless and obscure.

Chris had to go on a journey inside and dig really deep to find meaning again in her life. By making that journey inwards she did feel again a connection with other people, with her life and ultimately with herself.

The stories of three women like this are interesting I think because everything in each story is true at some level and yet they all tell a story about the same woman. I know this because they are all my stories. But doesn't each one tell a slightly different story?

I know that for me even reading over these little snapshots each one conjures up a different feeling and emotion and although I recognise things in them I have a slightly different sense of myself with each one. I can see the labels and the stories that were given to me.

Even the titles of those stories – Plain Jane – why is she plain? Because she doesn't look attractive, because she loved motherhood or because she suffered from depression? Did you feel sorry for her or were you irritated by her? More importantly am I irritated by her? What if the story had been called Plain John?

Words are very powerful and the verbal reasoning part of our brain soaks up words like a sponge and they then go some way to make meaning in our brains. What about the particularly emotive word 'lesbian' in Chris's story? Shocked, intrigued or did you think it was just stereotyping or more importantly to me, limiting?

How we choose to tell the story of our lives has a huge effect on how we see ourselves and ultimately how we experience our lives.

A metaphor in NLP is any story used to illustrate a point or idea. As already described, storytelling is an age-old tool used to impart wisdom, and stories also connect with both the conscious and unconscious parts of our minds. As a listener you identify with a key character, which helps you to accept the key message of the story. While facts and explanations may cause your mind to wander from the subject, stories are easy for the unconscious mind to remember.

Metaphors can highlight hopes, beliefs, anxieties and solutions and are a wonderful way to bypass the conscious mind and help us to invent our own solutions for change. As you already know the best stories capture the imagination and provoke us to look at a situation in a fresh way or do something that we might not otherwise attempt. They can inspire us.

Storytelling Exercise

Now, what is your story? Taking time to actually catch what it is you tell about yourself can be very revealing.

Find a space and some time to yourself and take a blank page of paper and 'free flowing' write out your story. Treat it like a story with a beginning, a middle and an end. Give it a title. Just put down whatever comes to mind about your story without censoring anything and see what comes out. Take at least 20-30 minutes to do this. If you seem stuck in a particular situation in your life at the moment, write that story. What exactly are you telling yourself about it? Let it flow...

Now go for a walk if you can. Or do something active like kick a ball around, do a workout or dance to some music that will get a rhythm going in your body to help change your brain state from one of verbal thought (more on this later, just trust me on this for now). Take at least 40 minutes for this before you read over your story and see if anything of interest has come up.

Take a look at the words, the metaphors you are using and ask yourself what happened in the story and what did you make it mean? Is it your story or did someone else give it to you? Were there labels you were given as a young child that, like the post-it notes, have stuck? Do you really believe these labels? Most important of all, could you tell a different story?

Awareness of how we are telling our story is a great place to find motivation for change. You can give up all the stories of limitation. There is a very useful NLP Storytelling Change exercise which involves you telling your story repeatedly with a number of different intentions to another person (the listener). These differing intentions help us to realise that a story is not reality, and that we have the power to re-evaluate the meaning of what has happened in our lives.

Storytelling Change Exercise

This is an exercise done with someone else and, like all NLP exercises, is better understood when actually practised than read about. The exercise involves you as a storyteller, and a listener who provides a human presence to witness the unfolding of the story and the changing perception of you as the storyteller. It can also be interesting for the listener to report their observations about how the story affected them at each telling.

1. The teller chooses an area of their life they would like to tell the story of and treats it like one with a beginning, middle and end.
2. The teller then recounts their tale with the aim of complaining as much as they can. If there is time allow the storyteller to complain until they are blue in the face!
3. The next telling has the intention of 'enrolling' the listener, of convincing the listener that the story is true and important.
4. The third time round the story is told as if pitching to a Hollywood producer. Who will play your part and the parts of any significant others? You can add a cast of thousands, a backdrop of your own choice and an unforgettable soundtrack.
5. The final telling of the story is given with the intention of serving the listener, to entertain and inform.
6. Feedback and debriefing part of the exercise – how has the sensation of the original problem shifted? Have any solutions presented themselves?
7. Now what story do you want to tell about the future, based on any insight, understanding or awareness the exercise has revealed?

As I will say repeatedly throughout this book our voice (and the words we use) is one of the most powerful manifestation tools we have. What we say to ourselves and what we say out into the world can change everything – we manifest what we speak.

Other Women's Stories

And what of the stories of other women's lives?

Think of the greatest stories – from the Bible, the great myths and legends, the great wars, the great writers and even the latest blockbusters or soaps, *particularly* the soaps – whose stories are they and who is making them? Where are the women's stories in these? And what exactly are the women doing in these stories? Are they strong, powerful and making great leadership decisions? What about in your own family – what are the stories of the women that are told? What did you learn about the women in the previous generations other than their marital status or the number, if any, of children they had?

I'm not going to go off on an exploration of the representation of women throughout the history of storytelling, religion or whatever. That's a different book entirely but I do want you to think about it for a moment and begin to notice in your everyday life which ones are being presented and talked about the most. Which are more available for you to be influenced by? How do you tell the story of other women – without judgement or criticism?

Who would you be if you gave up all the stories of limitation and got yourself a different story?

CHAPTER FOUR

The Long Arm Of Executive Function

Do you ever feel you are watching your life like it is your very own soap opera and you are the main character? From an elevated vantage point you can see the struggles, the interactions, the failed attempts at making sense, the joys and the longings that make up your life lived out in front of you. On certain days you want to reach down and adjust the course with a little nudge, on others with a swinging, thumping arm…

We women have very big brains. It's a part of being human and baby humans are unique in the primate world in that our brains, although huge by comparative standards when we are born, go on developing long after birth. It takes a lot of energy to feed that developing brain and to manufacture complete 18-year-olds by which time we are allegedly adults. Our big brains and the bodies that contain them need two things to develop – energy (or food to make that energy), and information, most of which is already there in the form of our genes, our DNA.

The rest we take in from our senses and those big brains then process that sensory input using methods such as filtering, deletion and distortion. If we didn't filter, delete or distort that information we would have sensory overload and we would never have time to make any meaning from the input we receive.

This processing, or psychology, is how we learn to talk, walk and interact with each other, balance our bank accounts, create works of art and take people beyond the thin blue line that surrounds our planet's atmosphere.

One reason that we humans are unique and only take our closest primate cousins as passengers on those trips to the moon and beyond is that we have the capacity to learn verbal language. It's the reason you can read and hopefully understand what I'm writing here and it is also the reason we can debate with our daughters and sons whether or not Joni Mitchell was in fact better than Bob Dylan, Madonna paved the way for Lady Gaga or after 30 odd years of listening to the reporting on the Northern Ireland Troubles I have yet to get a definition of the term 'family man' and what relevance it had to anything newsworthy. But I digress.

Another way our vast brains are unlike other organs is the way in which a brain reacts and responds to its subjective perception of the body in which it inhabits – it is self-aware. How we think we look, for example, will have a big effect on our self-image, attitudes and thought processes. We women are very aware of how we perform in comparison to our social neighbours. Our perception of ourselves in relation to other people continuously moulds how we think and feel about ourselves and this can be both motivating and limiting, particularly for women.

Neuroscientists are continually improving their understanding of exactly how this interaction or self-awareness actually takes place biologically and psychologically – what it is that makes us, well, human. From understanding how we form neural connections throughout both the white and grey parts of our cerebral matter to the geographical regions and parts that are stimulated when we form memories, fall in love or have a midlife crisis.

The good news is that the latest big brain ideas are hopeful in their conclusions in that we can change how we think about things, how we see ourselves and ultimately how we experience our lives. We can nudge and we can thump with that swinging arm...

Neuroplasticity, for example, is the brain's ability to re-organise, break old neural links and form new neural connections throughout life. It has been long known that neurons that wire together, fire together. Like a groove made in a folded piece of paper our brains form neural pathways that strengthen with use. What has been laid down in those grooves in early life had been thought of as hard or impossible to break but more recent knowledge about how the brain functions leads to the 'plastic paradox' – how the brain strengthens old, rigid patterns of behaving but that it can also be self-contradictory and generate new and flexible behaviours throughout the lifespan. Just as well.

Another big brain idea that I love is the *Left Shift*. Certain parts of the left hemishere (the left frontal cortex) are associated with feelings of caretaking, empathy and compassion. When activated they allow us to be relaxed and open to the world. Treating yourself with kindness will stimulate this part of your brain (the left shift) creating a state that is correlated with feelings of resilience and well-being.

The *Executive Function* of the brain is that part which coordinates, regulates and integrates the different structures and systems of the brain to allow us to make sense of our world, to learn and to use decision-making skills. It also gives us a smooth on-going sense of ourselves with our own personality, goals, values and skills. Yes, a smooth on-going sense of ourselves. Hmmn.

I love the concept of the Left Shift the most. That we can trigger and activate an openness and resilience to the world by treating ourselves with kindness and compassion is fantastic. Our brains and our minds have such a capacity for intuitiveness and an ability to find meaning in the depths of despair that it brings hope to the worst of situations. That ultimately we are able to change our neural pathways and our lives.

So how do we do this? Here's the nudge. The brain has different states and when in different states we have different outcomes in terms of our thought patterns, our behaviour and our experiences. Knowing and understanding these states is a powerful way to make change, experience life differently and ultimately to gain a clarity about who we really are underneath all the biological wiring.

Getting Into A State

When we are feeling 'bad' or 'low', irritable or fussed, a useful tip given to me was how it's good to just say HALT – before sounding off to anyone in earshot or reaching for the paracetamol – check first are you Hungry, Angry, Lonely or Tired? Our hormones and their fluctuation can also play havoc with our bodies, changing blood sugar and cortisol levels which, when combined with our obsession with so-called rational thought, can lead to negative or alarmist thinking.

Pay attention to your physical and emotional pain without trying to avoid the feeling, or thinking you 'should' feel different. Do what your body and brain want and surrender to it. It is this non-resistance that often deals best with whatever it is and allows it to pass more quickly.

The brain itself has different states too – resting, thinking, right brain, left brain and even verbal.

As mentioned before one of the things that separates us from the rest of the primates is our ability to use verbal language. In her book Finding Your Way In A Wild New World, Martha Beck describes how 'wordlessness' is the brain state that is the most important skill to attain for any wayfinder in any culture and any situation.

"I spend a lot of time talking about the reasons for my

clients' emotional swings and their life choices, but I have learned there are two ways to make such a choice: from a place of verbal thought, which has very little effect because it isn't rooted in their deepest perceptions, and from a place of Wordlessness, which makes every thought and action much, much more powerful. If you drop into Wordlessness, you'll be so aware of your situation and your own responses to it that you'll go towards your best life, no matter how obscure it may seem or how many obstacles lie before you. At a time when social change is so rapid and the pressures on people so unpredictable, Wordlessness is a skill you truly need to find your way."

So what does she mean by Wordlessness? Well, as said before our culture and our hard wiring means that we process and learn mostly by using words in a verbal language. To navigate fully in life, Martha believes, or when making decisions or trying to bring about positive change we need to move our basic perceptual and analytical thinking out of our heads and into the whole 'mind space' of the body. In other words, silencing the thoughts in our heads and opening to the experience of our body and our emotions. Or, if you prefer, thinking with our hearts and not our heads.

This is how she believes we begin to find our way through a terrible loss, a fulfilling career, a complicated relationship or a broken heart. Generally we cover up the directional cues of our physical and emotional experience with verbal thinking and if we can drop out of that way of using our brains and put the brain in a rest and relax state, magical things can occur.

So, if we change our state we can change how we feel about ourselves and our situation and there's more about how to do that in the next chapter. Before that, let's look in more detail at another nudge we can make by exploring how exactly we are filtering and distorting the sensory information we receive to make meaning in our minds.

One of the NLP presuppositions, or guiding principles, is that everyone creates mental maps of the world – that is, we make our own interpretation of how the world operates, and each of us has a different map. However, in NLP the map is not the territory. These mental maps, like a more traditional map of, for example, the Mourne Mountains, are only constructs; they're not the real thing. Just as we can't carry the entire richness of detail of the mountains to include absolutely every geographical feature in our minds, nor can we process every piece of information coming from our senses as we go about our lives and so we create an abstraction, a map. We do this via processes of generalisation, distortion and deletion.

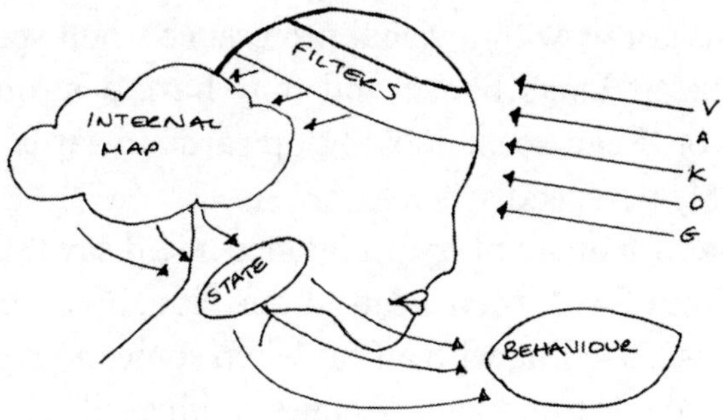

The Map Is Not The Territory

We receive information through our Visual, Auditory, Kinaesthetic, Olfactory and Gustatory senses which moves through our filters e.g. values, beliefs, deletion, distortion and generalisation to make an internal map made up of pictures, sounds, feelings, tastes and smells. This in turn influences our physiology and mental state and ultimately our behaviour.

We then create an internal representation from this somewhat reduced input – the pictures you see and sounds you hear in your head or the feelings that are generated within you. This in turn influences our physiology and mental state, how our mind and body react to new information and how we then behave – we create a state of *being* that is a combination of our mental and physical states and we behave in response to that state.

Changing any one of these three things (our physiology, our behaviour or our mental state) can change how you experience life. For example, if you feel anxious, this feeling affects what you observe, the words you say and the sound of your voice.

We, As Individuals

We each also have *default* states, and *primary* senses that determine what we pay attention to and how we as individuals prefer to think. Yes, that smooth on-going sense of ourselves. Often the language we use, both verbal and body, can give us clues to our preferred state. Do you for instance see, hear or feel? Those of us with a visual preference when speaking use terms like 'It looks like...' and may have a strong upright posture, or 'I can see...' looking upwards towards the sky or ceiling, 'My perspective is...'

Those with an auditory preference might say things like 'It sounds like...' with their head to one side, 'I can hear...' 'My question is...' leading with an ear when someone is speaking.

Kinaesthetic preference people say things like 'It feels like... ' 'I can touch that' 'My emotional reaction is...' and often like to hold onto something, like a pen, when talking and so on.

Filtering

Knowing now that we make these maps and how important they are in determining how we go about experiencing our lives, let us look a little more at the filtering our brains do with all that sensory input they receive. Although a fantastic mechanism to help us make meaning, the systems can sometimes develop patterns that are unhelpful to that messy, confusing and emotional life we have already alluded to. When life becomes confusing, difficult or overwhelming it can be useful to challenge some of our assumptions and beliefs and create new and better maps.

Deletion allows the conscious mind to ignore a mass of incoming information and has the benefit of letting you cope with the remaining messages. The downside is that you may selectively delete information that may be useful to you. We may become used to fuzzy thinking and speaking, habitually deleting important detail. This is often noticed in the vagueness of speech – missing information such as 'it won't work' (what specifically won't work?); a missing or vague subject: 'people say it's wrong to do that' (which people? do what?); using the passive voice: 'I was pushed' (who by?); fuzzy comparisons and unsupported judgements: 'I am rubbish' (compared to who? or what?) These hidden unrealistic comparisons are often preceded with words like 'obviously, or 'clearly…' Obvious to whom? What is 'obvious' to one person is not necessarily obvious to another.

When we group a range of happenings under one heading we are making a *generalisation* – we label information and slot it into categories so that your conscious mind doesn't have to cope with too much difference. We make generalisations so we can make rules, without which the world would make little sense and be almost impossible to live in. Children learn and develop their skills through this technique so that they do not have to cope with too much difference – if they didn't they would have to invent a new word for every object or experience they ever had.

Again though, generalising can be limiting, making us rigid in our thinking and unprepared to notice exceptions to the rules. We eliminate choice and opportunity by assuming that a past experience will be repeated in the future ('I was dumped in that relationship therefore I will be dumped in all future relationships').

The third way the brain filters information is by *distortion*.

We distort reality to suit our need for comfort, predictability and to save time. It is like we have the wrong lens on a camera and we assume causality where none exists or we assume we know what others are thinking ('they're angry, I must have done something wrong') and we dress up opinions into facts ('women like us don't do that sort of thing').

Distortion is a positive and necessary part of any creative or artistic process but as you can see there can be a downside if we draw a conclusion that has a negative or limiting effect.

These unconscious filtering processes are all happening within a matter of seconds and in order to take any control of the system we can begin by creating an awareness. Begin to notice deletions, generalisations and distortions by listening to your language. The words you use can give you vital clues. If you hear yourself using phrases like 'I've seen this before', 'I've done it again', and words like 'everyone', 'people', 'always', and 'never', you could be generalising. Take a look back at the story you wrote about yourself – anything of interest there? Ask yourself, 'how is it different this time?'

One Giant NLP Experiment?

Remember too that a lot of the learning and messages we receive come from our parents who are already living and breathing examples of their own filtering processes. As too are the swathes of media and advertising representation we are continuously subject to that I talked about in chapter one. Society and culture can be seen as one big NLP exercise in conditioning our thinking! As I have said before if we're not hearing or seeing positive messages we can grow into adult women with a limited belief in our own capabilities.

As adults we are tempted to think those early beliefs about the world that we take on are tempered and informed by later experiences. That as we get older we become worldly wise and able to see all the facts about things to make more balanced opinions. In fact, what happens is that we become selective in the information we take in (we delete and distort) and use only that information which *reinforces* our original beliefs. In other words, beliefs help create the reality around us, and we act accordingly to the reality we have created. ('We see what we want to see', 'perception is reality', 'what we think about, we bring about'). This is how prejudices can be formed and reinforced as we seek out information to confirm our beliefs or to confirm our own story about ourselves.

What We Think About, We Bring About

Going back to my own turmoil described earlier, when I turned the key and walked through the front door of the house I did finally manage to buy, I stepped in and fell down a previously unseen black hole in the floor. I walked around the rooms and I cried and cried. I truly sobbed. It was absolutely everything I did not want. It had creaking old floorboards, dowdy decor, was draughty, none of the doors fitted properly, hardly a light fitting worked and the kitchen was like something that was once functional in the 1970s. *I* now felt old and cold as I walked through those rooms and it was like *I* didn't fit anywhere anymore. I was distraught.

What I in fact had was the most overwhelming manifestation in the real world, of everything I had thought in my mind that I *didn't* want in a house.

Repeatedly thinking about something, even if it is what you don't want to have, is more likely to bring it into being – remember we get more of what we focus on and if we are thinking about what we *don't* want, usually as a way to avoid it, we are more likely to bring that about.

What is your default thinking pattern? What is your motivating energy? Fear? Love? Do you have a positive focus? Be mindful of where your focus of attention is. Remember, energy goes where attention flows...

Before getting bogged down in the worry about how we women ever make meaningful relationships or achieve great things remember that on the whole these processes are beneficial to us and it is really only if we are experiencing some difficulty in our lives or know there is something we would like to achieve or improve that it can be useful to examine what and how we are doing what we do.

NLP coaches can help their clients gain greater clarity about their situation by exploring how they create their maps and by using the unconscious mind as a tool to expand these mental maps. They can use what's called the Meta Model as a tool to ask powerful questions and listen to the answers they receive to understand how their clients are filtering information and to challenge some of the unhelpful distortions and generalisations they are making. They can also help their clients to change their states and show them how by doing that you can create new possibilities and bring results.

The Life Reconnected process also uses this understanding of how we use our brains to make sense in our worlds and how we can bring about shifts in both our thinking and experiencing. This leads us nicely to the second part of the book which describes the Life Reconnected principles for making creative change in our lives. How we can develop possibility consciousness by employing that swinging, thumping arm...

PART II

The Beautiful Game of Life Reconnected Principles

CHAPTER FIVE

Tipping The Happy Balance

Mind the gap and stay modern. By connecting both parts of our brains and brain states, i.e. when we balance our minds, we can access our own intuition and the inner voice speaks

A Life Reconnected finds balance between the chaos and order, the transitions and the plateaus, the renewal and repeat. Change is certain and welcomed. Embrace the new. Who are you going to be and how good were you yesterday? It doesn't matter. Your life is here for you now. The process of change is like everything else, a balance. The right brain gazes forward with the quality of imagination and the left analyses back through memory. Two great spurs of rock-hardened processing that need to be anchored to each other to form meaningful change. Live your life grounded in the gap inbetween. Find the balance between making something happen and letting it happen. Make the map and take it with you but enjoy what you actually see along the way.

I am standing on the Giant's Causeway World Heritage Site on the North Antrim coast of Northern Ireland. The place is absolutely magical. A cacophony of sound, colour and movement as I look out across the ocean and feel a rumble of energy stirring underneath my feet. Great solid columns of cracked black basalt stretch out to the right and left of me and the sea is bubbling up like a cauldron of thoughts repeatedly crashing over the shoreline as if it needs to drive home a message.

The Giant's Causeway and surrounding area is steeped in mythology and folklore, the Tourist Board desperate to widen the appeal as much as possible. I too have heard the stories of the feuding giants, one in Ireland, the other in Scotland and the potential breaching of the Causeway between the two. I have also learned about the geographical explanation for the unusual rock formations involving the cooling of molten rock to form the hexagonal columns now exposed after millions of years of erosion from that relentless tide.

I have been up to the Causeway twice before in recent years and earlier today I could feel the excitement rising again in my belly like a child going on a first trip to the seaside. Both times before I felt sheer enjoyment, pleasure, a communing with the natural environment that seemed to fill my boots as I stood gazing out at the constantly moving ocean or walked over the footsteps of the giants and those world famous columns. But not today.

Then, I had the people I love most in the world stepping over the stones with me but on this day I feel a different feeling. Less the lightness of before, more an internal churning similar to the sea and that old familiar tug of loss bubbling up within.

When I get home I look at a photograph of myself standing on the stones. I look like any other tourist, enjoying the outer landscape all the while my smile belies my inner sadness. Then I see something else. I get the message.

It's a personal reflection of my life. I see that even a rock solid base with time cannot escape the changes brought about by the swirling, lashing, ebb and flow of a life. To walk in the footsteps of the giants, even to stand on their shoulders, requires the courage to know that everything changes, hearts do heal and that I need to be thankful for the small but meaningful life I have and the opportunity to just let the wave crash over me once again.

I just need to keep my balance.

"There is a road from the eye to the heart that doesn't go through the intellect"

Have you ever made a vision board? You know the representation of everything you want in your life? It helps to connect the right brain (and our unconscious) with the left (our more ordered conscious brain) using a visual stimulus. Music also helps engage the right brain as does colour. I made one.

So what exactly was I doing creating a vision board? Well as I have described before when I was in the depths of despair I really believed I didn't like anything in life; that there was nothing I loved or wanted to do and that I had absolutely no control over what was happening now or in the future. I felt empty, lost and like I would never again enjoy anything. It was like all the joy had been sucked out and all that was left was the empty shell of a person and a life. Shame on me.

"But you can do anything you want", "You have no distractions now, do whatever you want", "What do you want in your life, really, what do you want?" These were all the things that were said to me. I wanted to kill myself, that was all. Well actually I didn't want to kill myself but like many others in a deep depression all that I knew I wanted was for the pain to stop and this life to stop. All the things that had brought me pleasure up to this point in my life felt meaningless, lacking in colour and content. Sad times.

Well, sometimes when you hit a wall you have to stop. You can't get through it or over it, you just have to stop. It felt to me like I had to go back to the beginning, the drawing board of my life if you like. So one day in a cold month that was February I got out my magazines, scissors and Blue Tack and I began to cut and paste in the old fashioned sense of the words. I let my creativity rip, tearing out any image that spoke to me on some level. I played an old favourite CD that I had avoided over the previous 18 months and I busied myself for hours plastering the whole wall of a spare bedroom. Really, *hour*s. I absolutely *enjoyed* myself.

But how could this be? What exactly is going on when we give ourselves the space to play? Are we lost in some time warp that takes us back to our childhoods? Is it the creative process that just overcomes us like a force coming through that is pure joy to experience?

Okay, engaging the left brain, it may be just that we have given ourselves space to 'think' our way out of our problem. I know it's not that. In fact it had been this wish to think my way out of the despair I was in that is exactly what kept me stuck.

No, there is something about the creative process, however naive and primitive it is, that lets us look through a window to see that we are so much more than we think we are. When we tap into the unconscious part of the mind and imagine, dream, draw, write, our worlds are suddenly so much bigger and full of possibility. It is like we have connected with our souls and the really funny bit? It is like we have tapped into a pool of *collected* creativity, the part that makes us human and that is what keeps us feeling connected to something bigger than ourselves. We can gain insights, fresh ways to look at situations and tap into an intuitive guidance system that is inside each and every one of us.

Breathe, Move, Play. Discover Yourself.

What we are doing is connecting somehow with the unconscious part of our brains. It is here that most of what goes on in our minds takes place. It operates 'out of awareness' and yet affects what we think, do, say and feel. We've already seen that our unconscious mind deletes, distorts and generalises sensory input. It controls our states, emotions and mental processes and it also controls our physiological systems such as our breathing, circulation of the blood and the nervous system.

Our unconscious mind is also the seat of change. By forming a mutual respect-type relationship with both our conscious and unconscious minds we can bring about the change we wish to see happen. Ask the questions you want to have answered and then pay attention to your intuition and your dreams. Spend time on activities that keep you deeply absorbed. Meditate, bake, write, play a musical instrument.

Other ways to drop out of our ordered-thinking brain state and balance the mind are doing anything that changes our breathing and our physical rhythm of movement. Dancing, running, relaxation and breathing exercises can all bring about a trance-like state to our minds (don't worry about the use of the word 'trance' here, I'm not talking about a zombie-like trance where you walk around with your arms stretched out in front of you. Although come to think of it that might actually do it...).

Martha Beck talks about the four Ds – Dancing, Drumming, Drinking and Dreaming that modern cultures all do to induce this feeling. Anything that involves trance and ritual will bring us to this state and subtly changing the inner life like this will begin to change your outer life too. My favourite one of all and a big part of the Life Reconnected process is walking.

Walking

Walking is one of the most powerful of mind percolaters.

Taking your 'problems' for a walk does many different things. It can get your body moving in a steady rhythm, it can get you to lift your eyes to a higher vantage point, it can change your breathing. Walking is the most natural and fundamental of all human conscious movements. By the simple act of putting one foot in front of the other and moving your arms in opposition you can propel yourself forward and gain not only momentum with a dynamic aerobic activity, but also a space for mindfulness. Walking with awareness in the present moment can open up that channel to the unconscious part of our mind.

For me, 20 minutes into a steady pace of walking and I begin to feel the magic. I'm tuning out my verbal thinking and tuning in to my sensory input. My lungs are expanding and I'm noticing things I didn't before. I hear more than the background chatter and I feel more than the warmth of my legs with every step. Even the grey sky can begin to take on a shape and form. I see symbols of meaning in all four directions and I feel a calming, restorative influence all around me.

I live in the city of Belfast. Northern Ireland is not known at first tell for its natural landscapes – the rugged coastline, ice-scarred rock formations and fabulous lakes even though we have all of these. More often we have come to be known as that place of the Troubles where people have been murdered for their political views and politicians are more likely to be heard using the tried-and-tested political strategy of 'stirring the pot of hatred' rather than say, forward thinking or even liberalism, conservatism or whatever. Well all that bores me witless and for most of my adult life I felt nothing but a disconnection from the place where I live. But even here I know there are two sides to everything.

When I get outside and even after only half an hour's walking from my home (remember the one with the black hole in the floor) I can get to a view point where I can see clearly for miles. Looking south I see the peaks of the Mourne Mountains bursting out of the horizon. Following the line of the hills as they sweep north towards Belfast I can see Slieve Croob, the source of the River Lagan that flows all the way to and through Belfast, where it meets the mouth of Belfast Lough.

West, out over the hills, lies a flatter landscape falling away in my view. The light from the sky falls strongest here as it is late afternoon. Walking on and looking east I can clearly make out Scrabo Tower, standing tall and proud at the top of the crag and tail glacial rock formation that guards the northerly shore of Strangford Lough, a diverse natural habitat, within which the tips of drowned drumlin hills create a myriad of islands.

Swinging back closer in my sights I can see the more jumbled landscape of the city skyline with the twin gantry cranes that have stood in the docks where the *Titanic* was built and launched. Even closer yet, behind a closed gate, a young foal stands on bending, swaying legs, eyes wide with wonder at the spectacle of me and my dog peering over the gate.

I stand with my head high and circle, taking in the four points of an imaginary compass and the wide wonder of my environment. When I take in this perspective my mind opens another gate, one to inspiration and all the answers I've been looking for seem to jump out.

Several years ago I went on a walking/coaching holiday to Spain and there I learned that we can 'flip' our situations to find the positive and that sometimes by just looking at what is in front of us we can get a cue.

I was reeling from my 'situation' as I described it then – heartbroken, bereaved, jobless and for want of a better description, homeless. And that is just the point, there is always a different description.

I can clearly remember sitting on a rocky overhang in the soaring heat looking all around me while in my mind I was unpicking my life. I could see that everything there had adapted and found its niche. The plants had somehow found enough soil to thrive in, the trees had grown tall enough to reach the light way above their rooted feet and even the scruffy dog that had followed us from the village raced around that overhang sure-footed and goat-like. I kept thinking, 'I need to find my niche. Where the heck is it because I feel like I don't fit anywhere anymore?'

What I could also see around me were the remains of localised rock falls and landslides where the ground had fallen away taking out everything in its path. A sure sign I thought, that everything does change, nothing stays the same and we can all get swept up by the force of it. So I tried to flip my thinking.

My father's death, in an unexpected way, had given me the opportunity to enjoy my mother's company more, to appreciate the time I have with her and to feel compassion for her in a way I had never been able to before (it even gave me an excuse to cry). My broken heart taught me that I need to show compassion for myself and that it is ok to feel a wholehearted love for someone else as long as we can feel it for ourselves.

My joblessness gave me the time to be with my family when they were in need and to take the time to really, really work out what it was I wanted to do.

Even on gloomier days now when the tops of my more local mountains are cloaked in low cloud, if I stand and look I will see something different. Here the light can fall in different spots highlighting (this time) buildings or reflections of water not noticed before. It might remind me that you can't always see what you want to see and that sometimes you just have to be patient and let things be revealed in their own sweet time. There will always be something to connect to.

I appreciate it all. These moments when I can give thanks, see the bigger picture and recognise that, like the waters in Strangford Lough, we all have hidden depths. That whatever we are struggling with in life, if we shift ourselves even just a little bit we will see something we've missed. Like the iceberg that the *Titanic* hit our unconscious mind is huge beneath the surface of our conscious one.

You might bump into that iceberg but it doesn't have to sink you. Everything, and I mean everything, balances out eventually. What was once big can become small and what was once limiting in our lives can free us to stand tall again and see the future all around us. We just need to walk into it.

Sometimes this is all we need to do in our lives. Get a different, more balanced perspective, a 360 degree view.

Honour and appreciate diversity. Accept it into your heart until it swells with gratitude and you will regain your balance. Make your map, your vision board of everything you want in your life but like any good navigator use all your senses. Look up from that map and around and appreciate what is actually here. Raise your awareness and live in the present.

24 Hours Of Possibility

Every single day is 24 hours filled with possibilities starting this very second. Remember, there's the life you planned and there's what comes next.

When thinking about the process of change you are going through recognise it is like everything else, a balance. Remembering also that when goal setting, the right brain gazes forward with the quality of imagination and the left brain analyses backwards through memory. Two great spurs of rock-hardened processing that need to be anchored to each other to form meaningful change. We have to learn from the past, visualise the future but live in the moment, now. Find the balance between making something happen and letting it happen. Like taking the map but enjoying what you actually find on the way.

CHAPTER SIX

Only Connect

It is the big 21st century quest, to be connected. It is an essential part of being human. Everything, and I mean everything, is interconnected.

A Life Reconnected is part of something giant. Like the honeycomb web of interconnected spaces found throughout nature, we are all connected. We need to reach across those spaces between us and make authentic connections with others. Like the queen bee you can show your colours, increase your circle of influence and then buzz off to a life filled with honey. Begin with what you have, what you are – small but valuable. Then, and only then, do you expand and become giant.

"Connection is why we are here. It's what gives purpose and meaning to our lives"

Brené Brown

When I was told to get up off my knees and see the green field that was my life I felt a disconnection with everything around me. With my life, my community, my purpose and ultimately with my own identity as a person. Set adrift from everything that had once held me, spinning but grounded, in my own little world, I was pitched into a dark place that I couldn't recognise.

I started writing. What began as a biography and then a memoir of a relationship quickly morphed into an exploration of homophobia and how it actually plays out in a person's life. It was trying to keep up with the force of change that was being driven through my life and as I sank deeper and deeper into despair it began to be my only way to keep connected with life.

When on the walking/coaching holiday in Spain I met a bunch of people from different parts of the world and I read a little of my writing to them. A little of the story of a woman trying to make sense of her life. I felt then that I was gripping on to that life by my fingertips knowing that I had to let go and reach out to something, someone or some thought that might offer a more secure place in my world. *"Falling is very scary, clinging on to life with your fingernails all the while trying to lift a hand off completely to reach out. To finally just let go and see if something might break your fall. Well, this is my landing,"* I read. They touched my heart in their response in a way that showed me there were still people in this world that I could connect with.

I came back from Spain buoyed by the connections I had made there and I began blogging. In my 'About' page I described the blog as 'an account of the experience of depression, partly a break-up survival guide and maybe even a midlife crisis tale.' Mostly though, it was describing a journey of hope.

I offered up my story in the hope that we connected as human beings through stories. People followed me as I attempted to rebuild that life. They read my posts and I theirs and I began slowly to feel connected once again to life. To get a window into other women's lives, some of whom live on the other side of the planet and to make meaningful connections with them gave me a space to piece together a sense of purpose, love and balance in my own world.

Shortly after beginning to blog I had a dream that I was on a bus and some guy cornered me and injected me with something. I was terrified. I had the feeling that he had done it before and then he did it again and I suddenly went all limp and sort of paralysed down one side of my mouth. I couldn't speak.

When I woke from the dream I thought about the fact that I had recently had radio iodine treatment for an overactive thyroid gland and guessed I was just reliving my fear of that. Over the course of the day I realised it was more the censoring part of the dream that was the strongest feeling I was left with. The fact that I had been silenced.

With Ourselves First, Then With Others

In her Ted Talk (Google this, you have to hear it) about connection and vulnerability, Brené Brown talks about how it is shame that perpetuates a feeling of disconnection in our lives. Shame, she says, is easily understood as the 'fear of disconnection'. That feeling of 'is there something about me that if people find out about it, I won't be worthy of connection?'

The things she can tell us about shame are that it is universal, we all have it, no one wants to talk about it and the less you talk about it, the more you have it. What underpins this shame is the 'I'm not good enough' and we all know that feeling – I'm not thin enough, rich enough, clever enough, 'fill in the blank' enough. What Brené found was an excruciating *vulnerability*. The idea that in order for connection to happen, we need to allow ourselves to be seen, really seen.

She goes on to describe how she went back to her thousands of interviews and deconstructed this knowledge about what she had found into two groups of people. Those who had a sense of love and belonging and those who struggle. She found one variable. The people with a strong sense of love and belonging believed they were *worthy* of that love and belonging. They had the courage to be imperfect, had compassion for themselves as well as others and they had a connection as a result of *authenticity*.

Those people who felt connected were willing to let go of who they thought they should be in order to be who they were and they knew that they had to do that for connection. Also, they fully embraced their vulnerability. They believed that what made them vulnerable, made them beautiful. Vulnerability was the birthplace of joy, creativity and love.

So, back to my dream. I really do believe that the crisis I had in my life was brought about by my lack of authenticity. My desperate attempt to hide that shame that I felt and had felt for most of my life. My own censoring of my inner voice that, I thought, spoke of the love that dare not speak its name – that of another woman. Rather, I realised and acknowledged it was a different love that I was suppressing – self-love. The belief that I was worthy of love and belonging.

When in Spain and then later in my blogging I was being truthful to other people about where I was in my life for the first time. I was describing my experience of the total loss of myself with an openness I never had before. Somewhere from deep inside me my unconscious was flagging up an illustration of the censoring I had been doing up until this point.

Ultimately, I believe we have to connect first to ourselves. Authenticity is inspiring. Be yourself, it is enough. Who are you comparing yourself to and why? Accept who you are and acknowledge that the vulnerable and beautiful mess you are inside is enough.

Then, when we have connected with ourselves we can make meaningful connections with others and that is what gives meaning and purpose to our lives. What we do does have an impact on people around us. We are all role models in our lives and it is important to look at how we can influence others. Let us be positive role models for younger women coming behind us, in how we are connected first to ourselves and then with others. As women we are inherently good at making those connections and in nurturing others. Be the change you want to see. Don't complain about other people, see their humanity and be a role model for them. Earn the trust of others. We are all spinning after all. Spinning and trying to stay connected.

With Nature

We also have to connect with the natural environment. We don't live in a vacuum no matter how many concrete walls we build. Nature is all around us and by being aware of the wonder and awe of it we are reminded at times when we are in pain, or hurting, or confused or when the winds of change threaten to blow us round the rooms or off the board of life, there is a greater driving force that we are all part of. It can be magical, and liberating.

Stand in front of an ocean for a while, sit outside on a seat in your garden or in a park or a field and just notice what comes up. I will guarantee something new and illuminating will. Look up at the night sky, even if you are in a city or town, look out the window and catch a shadow or a bird, a moon and even a star. Get a window on the world. Create that space for you to have it. Find your legal route to awe.

Encourage nature and wildlife in your life if you can. Put up a bird feeder, garden, or just be more observant any time you are outside. I am not ashamed to say that when I was feeling really low I found comfort in the Black More fish called Thompson that came to stay with us for a while. I found the constant will to keep swimming curiously inspiring as I watched and the graceful fins seemed almost to be waving at me.

The bird feeder and fat balls I put outside the Hammer house of horrors I described earlier, during the coldest winter for 40 years, repaid me in spades the following spring with a gorgeous family of sparrows all through the following summer. They never left my garden. Proof indeed that I could still have an influence.

Interestingly this year I have had nesting swifts, very unusual, in the gable wall of my neighbour's house. I have been able to stand and observe these aerodynamically crafted birds as they display their amazing turn of speed and gliding efficiency. I tell myself they too must detect my benign presence.

Walk outside, take a 360 degree view and get a new perspective on your life. Start with what you see closest to you then expand outwards and feel the connections. Like a wonder cure, if you can connect with the big outdoors and nature your situation will get some soothing.

Find your own natural connecting space and visit it often. The changes may seem slight at first but they will gain momentum until one day you look and realise that you are thankful for all the spaces of magic in your life both small and big.

With Our Lives

If we can do all of these – connecting with ourselves, with others, with nature – then we bring about the greatest connection, that of ourselves to our lives. If we feel out of whack or sync in one part of our lives it can affect how we are in others. When we connect, authentically, with our lives then they become lives well lived however we choose to spend our time.

CHAPTER SEVEN

You're Perfect!

Love, Oh Love – It's a Gift and Only When We Feel It For Ourselves, Can We Give It To Others

A Life Reconnected sees the beauty and awe all around us. Seek out the humanity, it's everywhere. See the small life detail, the tiny spaces of magic. Be life curious and see the beautiful mess inside each and every one of us and when you gaze upon that, you will feel nothing but love. As women, when we love ourselves with a wholehearted compassion everyone benefits. Our love expands and we can then give it to someone else in a way that it gets reflected back to us a thousand times.

As women we are constantly giving love and expressing our nurturing souls. We love our partners, our children, our families, our friends and their friends. Sometimes we forget to love ourselves with that wholehearted compassion we talked about in chapter six.

We need to love with our whole hearts and be willing to take the chance and say 'I love you' first to ourselves and then to others. To find that love is really all around us – we already have it and when we access it from inside we can feel it everywhere and spread it around.

A Word About Heartbreak

This is one I know something about. The all-encompassing longing and hurting and believing it will never be resolved. 'Life can never be that good again.' To think you have lost the one person that made your life complete. What was told to me I'm telling you now, hold on to your feelings. You will be ok.

In my frustration and hurt and anger, I believed that the only way anyone ever recovered from heartbreak and felt good about themselves again was to be in another relationship. For someone else to make them feel special again, lovable, and not be that person who would forever walk around with the word 'dumped' etched across their forehead.

Stories of how people, and particularly women, moved on in their lives after a breakup or life crisis irritated me to the point of denial as they seemed to confirm my belief that they only recovered when they were in another relationship. How quickly that ship sails again I wailed.

Even Elizabeth Gilbert, in Eat, Pray, Love annoyed me as the ending seemed particularly Hollywood Rom/Com-friendly (how psychic of me don't you think?). My other bible at the time, Shoot The Damn Dog by Sally Brampton, also ended with her in a new relationship so I decided these books made better coffee tables than guidebooks on ways to live your life, as I stacked them artfully beside my bed.

But I was missing a point. A chance observation by a dear friend reminded me that the story she told me of her friend recovering from a complete meltdown, including a psychiatric hospital stay, after her husband left her included a step *before* her next relationship. She had recovered from her deep depression. She made her own journey to a life reconnected.

My friend is also the most 'complete' woman I know, happily single, and surrounded by love.

I thought as a mother that the greatest pain I could ever feel was that of being separated from my children. Like being primed for the forces to come I can remember clearly, just hours after my first child was born, the overwhelming pang of that physical tug as the midwife took my baby away to another room to be weighed. It was all-consuming and went some way to ensure I would deliver any subsequent babies at home.

Later, with a shared parenting arrangement to accommodate our newly hatched way of living as separated parents, I felt that tug again as my now teenage children left me to spend time with their dad. But all that heartbreak and priming didn't protect my poor heart when it broke open and spilled out its contents for all to see some years later. It was more like my heart had been tipped up and a store of hurt had come pouring out.

This time, and each with a child's hand, my children reached out to me as they could see how small their mother had become. They demonstrated their love to me in ways that in my tortured state I was aware of even if I couldn't respond to it outwardly. Love expressed is love indeed.

I thought that I was afraid to express that I had loved and lost a woman and I had loved and lost a parent, but the pain led me to turn inside to find the real love I had kept hidden, that of myself. That love, when found, is never lost.

It makes you feel good about yourself and stops you comparing yourself to others. It gives you strength to just be yourself and know that it is enough and it makes life much, much more simple. If something feels out of whack in your life ask yourself, how would it be different if I really, really loved myself? If it didn't matter what other people thought because you know that you are already perfect?

Craft A Life Full Of Love

For it is only from here that I believe we can go on and make meaningful relationships, romantic and otherwise. There are many types of love in this one and whacky life that we have and none are so attractive as the woman who loves herself. Say goodbye to 'I have nothing to wear' – self-love is every season's must-have.

It is ok to be single and discover who you really are. Make your best relationship the one you have with yourself. It will be the most enduring and the most influential. In fact, it is essential to know and love yourself before making meaningful and lasting relationships with others.

Yes, love needs to be expressed, declared and ultimately felt. And when you do find it within it is unconditional. Not subject to promises fulfilled, behaviour displayed or even loyalty endured. I believe this is the greatest love and also the most challenging for us. We are told from a very young age to love our parents, our brothers and sisters, God, our partners, our children, our pets etc., but rarely ourselves. We are brought up to believe that that is selfish and yet it is the very key that unlocks the door to all other love relationships.

Remember the Left Shift from earlier – treating yourself with kindness creates a state of empathy and compassion. You will know you have it when you see the humanity in another person. The kindly act, the helpful hand and the words of support. The unselfish care that goes out like a wave and radiates back, expanding farther than the intended recipient. You'll see it and feel love all around you.

CHAPTER EIGHT

Follow Your Nefertiti's Nose To Find Your Bliss

> A Life Reconnected is powered by a vision of your own making. Being creative again and again lets you lose yourself to something bigger. Take directional cues from your complete physical and emotional navigational system. Breathe, move, play. Discover yourself. Awaken mind, body and spirit. Your vision plays from your heart, finds your place and connects you to your purpose so you can take it to the world…

Just 26 minutes of steady walking from my front door I can see Napoleon's Nose looming at me from under the clouds. A rocky outcrop of basalt that edges the top of one of the hills, Cavehill, surrounding Belfast, it is so-called as it is meant to bear a likeness to Napoleon Bonaparte in profile and he was, well, known to have a bit of a hooter. The story goes that Cavehill also inspired the story of Gulliver's Travels and today it is inspiring me to find my purpose.

As I ascend the quite steep incline the dark contoured outline forms the backdrop to my laboured breathing and I am unexpectedly reminded of how my dad used to say that I looked like Nefertiti, the Ancient Egyptian Queen, because a little replica iron bust he had of her, which used to sit in our fireplace, showed quite a big nose in profile too.

Less than half an hour ago I was in a feeling of overwhelm and disconnection, lost to a thought process about what I am doing in my life and why I am unable to capture and hold at least one of the creative ideas I am coming up with. Now with legs stretched and lungs expanded my body is moving in a rhythm that allows my wild verbal thinking to still. Suddenly my peripheral vision is picking up Nefertiti who seems to be saying 'follow your nose, follow your nose'. Begin with what you know and who you are, you'll find your bliss...

Time To Fess Up

What is your purpose? I mean what is your soul calling you to do? Do you know? Think you have an inkling? My guess is that if you only have an inkling then that's what you will have in your life – an inkling of what you are that feels like something is missing, or not yet begun, or waiting on some magical time in the future when the stars will be aligned before you can start. Is there a sense that inside there is something you are afraid to fess up and state, clearly, loudly, that describes what it is you really want to do or be? Do you even know where exactly inside you are experiencing that inkling, that knowing?

Finding and following that purpose is an essential part of being human and as we have already learned another essential part of being human is that life is messy and everything changes. When did you last ask what it is that you really, really want to do with your life? What, never? Someone must have asked you what you wanted to be when you grew up. Did you become it? Are you living it? Well, I'm asking you now, what do you want to be now you are grown up?

There are a few pointers to consider here before we set you off on your Life Reconnected journey to follow your own Nefertiti's nose and answer the calling that is there for you.

Firstly, being fuzzy about what you want in life brings you fuzzy results.

Secondly, no one else can decide for you what your calling is. They may be able to give you pointers but only you know what it is that will make your heart sing and pull you along when the going (or distraction) gets tough.

Thirdly, you have to do a little work here. It's an inside job and requires you to be very honest so is best done quietly, with yourself until you feel you know intuitively that you have accepted what that internal voice is telling you about your purpose. It isn't about figuring out the how, it's about figuring out the what. For some this is a very spiritual calling, for others it wells up from some other source all together but for all of us when we feel it, align with it and choose in favour of it, our lives seem to magically open up to all sorts of new and wonderful possibilities.

So, ask yourself, how do I find:

- My soul ambition, my mission, my reason to get up every day, my 'thang' that makes me feel complete, at peace, on purpose, inspired?
- The thing I am willing to go through fear and vulnerability for?
- The thing that when I do it people will be drawn to me?
- The thing that when my strength fails or I have a 'no, no' moment, it feels like it is bigger than me and so pulls me back and I keep going?

You can start very simply by asking yourself: what am I passionate about? What do I really, really love doing? What am I doing when I don't notice time passing and I'm in the 'flow'? What am I truly thankful for in my life? What do I believe in? What is my dream? Remember we are looking for feeling answers here not thinking, verbal brain answers. If the answers to these questions don't come immediately to your consciousness or you find yourself saying things like 'I know what I want but I know I can't have it' or 'I haven't noticed anything I enjoy doing for ages' then you are using the verbal part of your brain to censor your answers and that's no good.

Several methods of 'goal setting' describe ways to take you through a scroll of questions to analyse what and with whom you were doing things you enjoyed. However, my belief is that you just need to access what you already know intuitively in your subconscious, not by thinking it out but rather by 'being' or accessing our 'wordlessness' state. It's what's in your muscle. A knowing in your whole body of what it is that brings you peace. The exercises we described in the previous chapters should have begun to awaken that knowledge within you.

Flipping

The truth is that 95% of the time most of us are thinking about and putting our focus and energy on what we are *against*. We talk about what we don't like doing or don't want to be seeing or having in our lives. We complain, we rant, we rave, we make changes, they implode and we make excuses and complain and rant again. We think we've worked out what it is we want and we set goals, we get distracted and we complain and rant and blah blah blah.

Some of us even think that having a purpose, a mission and even goals are for those corporate giants that decide whether this year's love will be a skinny latte or a self-cleaning icar (only a matter of time...).

What those successful corporate visionaries have worked out though is that *clarity* is the stepping off point to getting what you want, going where you want to go and probably most important of all knowing when you have got there.

Another way to find your mission is to look at that 95% of our focus – i.e. what it is that we are against. Margaret M.

Lynch describes this so effectively when she calls it 'doing battle'. What is it we spend our time battling against? What are we defensive about? Your defence is what you are against and it is the way you battle. This is really important, especially for women who often feel disempowered, because when we are in battle we are *resisting* our power and our mission often by being distracted by others. What we are in battle about is often the exact opposite of what our mission or purpose actually is. We must uncover and clarify it so we can challenge it and flip it to find what we are *for* – and be that.

So, to find your true mission, again take some time and space to yourself and begin by asking yourself:

What do I spend my time battling? What cracks me up? What do I find so irritating? Unjust? It may not even look like battling but it is when you are doing things like:

- Achieving to prove your worth (instead of the love of pure expertise)
- When you are being ruthless and your inner critic tells you 'I should have known/done better'
- When you are judging and dismissing others
- When you are insisting you are not annoyed or angry: 'That doesn't bother me' (but you are in *total* judgement of someone or something they've done)
- When you are pushing and exhausting yourself (your body will eventually tell you)

When you are judging others as idiots it translates to "I haven't proven *I* deserve it yet."

When you are in battle you have decided imperfection is 100% true and that this person is it.

And there is nothing you don't see in someone else that isn't *you*. You're seeing something in them that you hate in you.

It can also look like:

- Being surrounded by people in your life who betray or disempower you
- Anger and resentment
- Complaining
- Day dreaming of 'them' getting their 'just desserts', the 'neh neh, ne neh neh' attitude
- Lashing out and attacking (How dare they?!)
- Self-recrimination, self-loathing and sabotage (no one even sees it, but you know it's there)
- Depression
- Self-medicating

When you are in battle you feel completely justified doing it – you get a momentary boost of power yes, but it is a negative pleasure. It feels good to rant and rave about injustice but truthfully it is coming from the dark side of you and won't lead to empowerment.

If You Are Not Allowing Yourself To Carry Real Power In Your Life You Will Take It In This Dark Side.

If you are a woman of achievement and you are not allowing yourself to be seen as the unbelievable, powerful and brilliant woman that you are then you have to get it from the list above or by telling people they are stupid and wrong.

If you are a charismatic leader (and we women have to own this quality) and you are not allowing yourself to lead in your life, to be the embodiment of empowerment in your life, to allow yourself to feel what Margaret calls the 'I rock', then you will go for it in the negative. You will get some group of people to agree with you and for 90 seconds you will be a charismatic leader. You will play small and not step up when an opportunity arises.

Your defence is also the thing you are
MOST,
AFRAID,
TO FAIL AT.

Think about this and ask yourself:

What does my lower self love about being in battle? Really step into a scenario where you are battling. Remember a time when you got really, really angry or mad or were in complete judgement of someone. How are you feeling? What are you saying and what is the other person doing? Then ask:

What is the pleasure?

What does it love about being in judgement?

What is the pleasure running through my body?

What does it really want and need?

If you can do this and be really honest with yourself you can capture and own something about yourself that is very powerful.

You Have To Follow Your Heart And Be True To Who You Are

Now ask yourself:

What is the light or flip side of this battle or judgement that I go into? Ask: what is it I am *for*? What people do I love? What is the thing that I am on this planet to embody, to stand as the living, breathing embodiment of this quality that is the thing I want to be seen for? What am I being called to do?

Take a deep breath, put your hands over your heart and hold that 'What am I for?'

Remember you can't get to it with your head – it has to come from the heart and it will feel way bigger than you.

If you step out of battle and be *for* something you become the change you want to see. Everything we do in the shadow will reveal a powerful gift in the light and to actually speak with your voice what it is you are for may be one of the most honest and soul baring things you have ever said to another person. You must speak it because your voice is the most powerful manifesting element you have. It is like a bridge – you 'speak' a thing and it starts to manifest. Manifestation starts when you speak what you want out into this world. So say what you are for, out loud and out often. Remember the power of the words you speak first into yourself, then out into the world. Your voice is your key.

As Margaret M. Lynch would say "Declare your freakin' mission, relentlessly!"

Welcome To Hollywood

Now you have accessed what your true calling or mission or purpose is we can begin our Life Reconnected journey to be the living, breathing embodiment of that purpose. You can let go of the resistance and step into being. You can feel the pleasure of carrying your own power. First, we're going to the movies.

> "*If there is a specific resistance to women making movies, I just choose to ignore that as an obstacle for two reasons: I can't change my gender, and I refuse to stop making movies. It's irrelevant who or what directed a movie, the important thing is that you either respond to it or you don't. There should be women directing; I think there's just not the awareness that it is really possible. It is.*"
>
> Kathryn Bigelow,
> First woman to win Best Director Academy Award in Oscar history, Feb. 2010. Her film, *The Hurt Locker* also beat *Avatar* to Best Picture that year.

One of the many visual elements that helps secure Bigelow's visual style as a film maker is her use of slow motion. This can apparently help us, the spectators, participate in a collective meditation on the action and affect (emotion) we are watching. We are now going to go on our own film maker's journey as a process to answer that 'calling' that we feel pulling our soul in a way that uses the Bigelow effect. We're going to slow our own movie down and help us participate in our own journey that connects our actions and our feelings, our emotions.

Story and movie makers from all of history have been demonstrated to use a formula or template to make a visual or audio narrative (story) that people can relate to. This template can also be used as a way to describe and bring about change in our own journey, to answer our calling; to step into being what it is we want to be instead of either knowing, describing or secretly wishing it were true for us.

And don't all movies or stories have a happy ending? (My jury is still out on E.T. – "Come" "Stay" forever etched in my mind as an insurmountable dilemma. I cried for three whole streets walking away from my first screening of it.)

What Does This Story Or Movie And The Metaphors In It Mean For You?

At first this exercise and the metaphors used in it may appear to hold no relevance to your life, but after a while, you may find that the characters, images and words are starting to mean something to you. Even if you don't realise it straight away, your unconscious enjoys working out what the story might mean for you and that in itself can bring new understanding. I have used this process in large and small groups and I have even taken myself through the process and each time it has brought revelations and new understanding. For some people it can be completely life changing.

How The Metaphor Is Processed

Metaphors engage the right brain similarly to dreams because they are symbolic and entertain as well as inform. We take what we want from the metaphor unconsciously and apply it to our own situation. Resistance to accepting the message is decreased because a story is much less confrontational than a direct statement addressed to the conscious mind. Within the content of the story you can present different points of view, suggest actions and propose solutions, and elicit any number of states – it provides sufficient scope to reframe you the listener, taking you from a negative state to an intermediate then a positive state.

The Hero's Journey

The simplified version of what has been found to be at the heart of all good stories and movies follows a pattern called the Hero's Journey. I have struggled to come up with a different title because I know that although the word 'hero' represents protagonists of either gender, for many people the word 'hero' conjures immediately to mind a male figure. Most of the original research into the theory behind this script used traditional stories that inevitably did have male heroes in them anyway. For those of us who know a thing or two about gender proofing and using gender neutral language, just to say that it can describe men and women doesn't really cut it. But then again neither does The Heroine's Journey – or does it?

Because I know the NLP process based on this to be quite a

powerful agent of change, I'm leaving it as the Hero's Journey for now and the more we identify with women as 'heroes' the more it really will begin to represent both genders. To make the point even more forcefully I see women as heroes in their lives every day and hopefully you will too. To labour the point to boredom levels I also have a bit of a problem with the word 'demon' in this exercise too but we have to get on...

So, what exactly is this Hero's Journey? The simplified pattern of the archetypal story includes seven stages:

- Hearing the calling
- Accepting the calling
- Crossing the threshold
- Confusion to clarity
- Gathering assistance
- The battle
- The return home

The story begins with the hero usually in a state or circumstance that is somehow unsatisfactory for them. They receive a calling to get up and do something about the situation. It usually means going on some sort of quest to find a solution.

Having decided to act our hero has to leave their existing world and cross a threshold into a new one where they will experience confusion. They discover the source of trouble in the world they have left is a demon of some sort and here in the new world it needs to be fought.

The hero knows she has to fight the demon and she also knows she needs to find help in the shape of another person or mentor. The mentor may provide some magical protection or knowledge that helps them to do battle with the demon.

The demon is finally confronted and overcome, not necessarily immediately, but often after some point of transformation for the hero when they learn something of immense value or undergo some personal change that allows them to turn things around and ultimately win the battle.

Often the demon is actually quite vulnerable and can even be co-opted as a helper for the hero who, in the final analysis, has come to solve a problem back in their original world. The hero has to get something from the demon, some kind of magic elixir that they can take back to fix the problem in the world they left behind.

In the end the hero returns with the elixir, delivers it and gets on with her life transformed.

Change Yourself: The Life Reconnected Hero's Journey Storyboarding And Casting

First we have to personalise this story and make you the hero. What is your calling? What are you for? Who are you becoming? What is the pain or hurt in your life, the world or the marketplace you need to solve? Are you being called to do something in your life? What will make you become fully alive in your life? If you are in the Change House, you, as the hero, start off in the Room of Denial, where you refuse the call, then move out of this room by accepting it until you reach the rooms of Renewal and Contentment.

Accepting the call means you have to leave your existing world where you are now, your comfort zone, and cross a threshold into a new place. Crossing the threshold is not the same as accepting the calling which is more of an internal shift. Rather the threshold is the thing that changes the world you are in that is irreversible (from here you cannot turn back – you've registered as self-employed, you've handed in your notice, you've got on a plane, you've signed a contract, you've told someone something...). Up until now you have always been able to stay put, from now on the only way is forward.

Is there something on the route to becoming your purpose that frightens, worries or is stopping you that will have to be dealt with at some point? What is getting in the way for you? What's the question you don't want to be asking yourself right now? Is there something undermining your morale or your self-belief? This will become the demon.

You're also the casting director in this movie so who are your mentors? You can have anyone you like whom can bring you the resources you need. People who maybe embody the qualities you will need. They can be characters from literature, the movies, people you know, people you don't but in whom you connect with some quality or strength you recognise in them.

The next part of the process is to go through a run of this journey using an NLP tool called a timeline. This is where we also employ the Bigelow effect. Reading and even doing this will seem a little odd but it can be a very powerful agent of change – as my NLP trainer used to keep barking, "Get on and do the process and then you can, if you still need to, ask why!" as we scurried off like naughty schoolchildren. The feedback afterwards was invariably about how revelatory the process actually was.

Finding a reasonably large space to work in you place yourself along a line laid out on the floor. Imagine this line as a span of time with the past at one end and the future at the other. Although not necessary, if you feel you need to, mark out the line with paper, or string if working outside.

Now place on your timeline, using bits of paper or other objects to represent them, in order:

The present: where you are now. As this is a forward-looking process, it helps to put this near the beginning of the line – i.e. have more future than past.

The threshold: not too far away from the present.

The demon: leave a bit of a gap between the threshold and

the demon as you will be placing your mentors here.

The point in the future where you have answered the call and have reached your goal with the elixir.

Mark a place beside but not on the timeline between the threshold and the demon for your mentors.

Directing

You are now ready to take yourself through the process.

Step up to the threshold and ask yourself, now you have accepted the calling how is the threshold stopping you? Imagine you actually have some physical barrier you have to push or squeeze through. Act this out, which may feel a bit odd, and as you are doing so think about what actually constitutes the barrier. What is stopping you from entering your new world? (This helps the unconscious mind communicate with you.) If working with a coach, they can role-play pushing past the threshold with you until you are through.

Then walk to the place you have put your first mentor. Step into their space and turn and face an imaginary you still on the timeline. Become the mentor (this is known as second position in NLP, yourself being first position), really taking on their body language, posture and facial expressions. Imagine wearing their clothes. Hear their voice. What are they saying? What are they offering you? You can imagine them actually handing you a gift or just saying something verbally to you. Again this is a way of letting that well-meaning unconscious communicate with you and you might be surprised at what comes up.

Step back onto the line as yourself and turn and face your mentor and receive the gift they have given you. Repeat the process for each mentor.

Next walk straight up to the point in the future when you have resolved everything and are living your calling. Walk past the demon as you do this. Standing at this point turn and face back down the timeline and ask yourself if there are any other resources you need to get through the threshold or to fight the demon?

If the answer is no then send all the gifts you have received down the timeline to your original self still waiting to cross the threshold.

If the answer is yes then imagine a mentor who can give you that quality and go back and carry out the mentor process again. Receive your new resource and walk past the demon again to the point where you have resolved everything and check again that you have all that you need.

Once you are sure you have all you need and have sent the resources back as gifts to you at your starting point, walk back beside, but not on, the timeline and, not treading on any of your mentors, go back to your original starting point. Stand facing back up the line and accept the gifts that you sent back from the point where everything is resolved (where you have the elixir).

Now, with all your resources and gifts within you make your way back up the line. Push past the threshold again, acknowledge your mentors and when you get to the demon, notice if it has altered in any way. There is often an 'aha' moment just now. Notice how it has changed – is it offering you any additional resource, insight you didn't have before? Has it changed shape or form?

Move the demon off the line and place it beside your mentors and step into the space and give yourself advice from their perspective. (One of the presuppositions in NLP is that every behaviour has a positive intention.)

Walk to the elixir point again, pause there for a while reminding yourself of all the resources you possess.

Finally walk back off the line to the start and walk slowly up the line to the elixir point again. Pause, then walk back off the line to the start. Walk slowly up the line again. Repeat this a few times until it feels as though the process has delivered all the awareness it can.

That's a wrap.

Whoever you are, be it. Being precedes all doing and to help you begin, follow your Neferititi's nose to the Life Reconnected process where you can do the casting and directing in your own movie and take your purpose to the world.

Part III

A Whole New Ball Game

CHAPTER NINE

The Life Reconnected Hero's Journey For Women
The Big Idea Condensed

"I like to see a person's sediment, to see traces of their past and reveal them. First and foremost though, I am contemporary and I love giving women the space for reinventing their lives for now. It is new, and it is powerful, and it is here for women to make the best investment they can – in themselves"

The Life Reconnected Programme Of Personal Change For Women

Life Reconnected holds that women are naturally creative, resourceful and whole. That they are completely capable of finding their own answers to whatever challenges they face. The purpose of the Programme is to ask powerful questions, listen and empower rather than instruct or advise. This in turn elicits the skills and creativity women already possess.

The training is both rigorous and fun and is where being and doing go hand in hand to foster growth. It takes the pyschological models described in this book and uses them in a way that relates to modern women's lives. The Life Reconnected Process is about letting go of preconceived ideas, rules and limitations and stepping into being who you really are, what is really important in your life and reconnecting with your purpose. It enables women to achieve success and fulfilment in their life through a powerful and dynamic group process.

It is also essentially a group process that brings about a journey of profound *personal* change. Effective learning involves both individualised training as well as benefiting from the strengths, experiences and contributions of others. Describing what actually takes place on a Life Reconnected Programme Of Creative Change won't capture the essence of how together women create a positive support environment, for the other women as well as themselves, in which to make meaningful change. You can't hear the laughter, see the tears or hear the clunk as the wheels of thought run free.

Also you have to actually practice these processes, you can't just read about and think about them using the verbal part of your brain. The focus is on participation and practical experience rather than lecture, with numerous opportunities to be coached and receive feedback. It needs to be 'in your bones' and an essential part of the Programme takes place walking (not too strenuous) outdoors in a scenic venue of the group's choosing.

There are huge benefits to group work, especially for women, both in sharing and presenting new role models. It is so important for women to find a space of their own, together. A space in which powerful, healthy conversations can unfold which can confront habitual thinking that stifles innovation and creativity.

Laughter happens in group work and laughter is one of the most powerful tools – it is the solvent of negative emotions. It relaxes us and helps to open the mind to new experiences without any fear of not knowing or understanding what is going on.

We can find our collective voice and start a new conversation about how women actually are already leaders in their own lives, and how we can reinforce that belief.

Creative change is a process that takes time. It is not necessarily an instant shift although there will be 'aha' moments along the way. All the exercises and materials have been designed to give women the best possible support through their own individual journey. Both the facilitator and other participants are witnesses to each other's transformation.

The Training Programme

The Life Reconnected Programme integrates the four principles described in this book that together enhance the quality and results experienced in each participant's life. Each of the four modules, taken in sequence, requires two days of training, allowing time for the processing of ideas. Each day is structured so that women feel they have time out from their busy lives to really dedicate to themselves, and that they are being treated and honoured in this time. Plenty of breaks, lunch and refreshments are included!

1. The Discovery Phase
   This module introduces participants to how we have got to where we are. How we process information and how we can ultimately bring about purposeful change. It also helps women understand that although they are uncomfortable, the states of chaos, confusion and inertia are all part of their forward motion. Topics include women and change, NLP presuppositions, an introduction to relaxation, balancing the mind and unlocking our creativity, and how we can get more from less in our lives.

2. Balance and Connection
   This module gives participants an opportunity to access

their own creative intuition, gain new and different perspectives and let go of limiting beliefs. It helps us to make use of all of our senses – to gain full sensory acuity and make powerful life choices and congruent decisions instead of dashing about at the mercy of circumstances. It includes one full day of walking and coaching and connecting with the big outdoors.

3. Finding Your Voice
   This module helps each woman look at the story of her life and discover for herself exactly what it is that is important. What it is that will bring joy and fulfillment. It will allow her to voice that purpose with confidence and so create a vision for a compelling future.

4. Directing Your Own Life Reconnected
   This module helps women to take their purpose to the world. It includes the Hero's Journey exercise described in chapter eight. How to find their natural sanctuary and other resources to support them as they go forward in their lives is another big part of this module.

Participants on each Programme can avail of follow up one-to-one coaching and a one-day Reconnecting and Celebration follows each full-length Programme, several weeks after it has ended.

Shorter 'taster' courses and individual coaching packages are also available based on the full programme as are group team-building and Life Reconnecting Days of Creative Change Solutions.

CHAPTER TEN

Being Part Of Something Giant

> It is so important to support and celebrate other women in our lives. Be the change we want to see in our worlds. Start a new conversation, one that moves women forward. Are you ready? Women, Think, Change…

I started off this book talking about the game of tennis and potatoes from an old game I used to play as a child. I'd like to end it by telling you that the game finishes with Seven Potato More! You can be more too and you can have a Life Reconnected.

I've Been Blogging Since You Left Me was one of the original title possibilities for my blog I talked about before. Along with *Dumped At Fifty, On The Scrapheap* and *Better Out Than In.* As I moved through trying to amuse myself to getting to the essence of what I needed to express, *A Design For Life* and *House, Job, Life* finally became *Life Reconnected.*

Then, I was sitting in that house I hated and feeling like I had a life I hated too. One that I couldn't control, recognise or find any purpose to. I was disconnected.

As I sit today in the front room of that same house I look out at the gorgeous view of two magnificent birch trees framing a small slice of a longer view to the mountains surrounding Belfast. The newly sprung leaves are dancing magically in the wind. Looking more closely in my sights I embrace the newly painted walls and the bobbing blackbird reflected in my shiny mirror. I feel my rapture at the patterns my fantastically cut light shade make on the ceiling above. I appreciate it all.

My lovely house swept white, clean and modern. My life swept clean and begun again reconnected.

I could just as easily called my blog *The Power of Words to Reconnect a Life* as it helped to bring about that reconnection, that feeling of being part of something bigger than ourselves. I have been on this journey and I know and have felt and lived the power of words to make change in our lives. Remember, the words we speak first to ourselves about ourselves and our story, and then to others can really be life changing.

You can do it too.

Making The Most Of Difference

If you think it is too difficult – it isn't. If you think your situation is too unique – it isn't. If you think you are too old, too young, and don't know where to begin, I can show you. If life has thrown all the balls up in the air and you are hurt, scared, heartbroken, bored or directionless come on this programme and get moving again in a way that feels joyful and inspired. Start a whole new ball game. Find that difference that makes the difference and make the most of it. This process works. It provides a toolkit and facilitates your journey to incorporate the four principles.

We are all connected, change is inevitable *and* we can support each other.

We can challenge what has gone before and create new role models both for ourselves and for each young woman coming up behind us.

There are also inspiring women's stories and role models out there if we look in another direction. Catch yourself, or anyone else for that matter, in being negative about women and their choices or behaviours. Be a cheerleader for women you know, see their strength and point out their achievements. See your own too. This message is to you if you are gay or straight, single or partnered, part of the Women's Movement or a member of the Women's Institute – we can all do better.

We are all role models and leaders in our own lives and if you are a woman of influence – a teacher, parent, business owner, trainer, policy maker or youth worker, ask what messages you are giving.

As women we are different from men and we can make the most of that difference for ourselves and for others.

A Note About Leaders

As I look around at the leadership we have had here in Northern Ireland I have no reason to doubt why we are afraid to step up. Why we hesitate and let others go first. It is very important for us here to get a window on the world and see that we are part of a much bigger community. If you can't travel out of Northern Ireland, travel with your mind and your heart.

We women are a gathering crowd. Come on and speak up. Let your voice be heard wherever you are in the world.

Find yourself someone to be your own cheerleader. Women need to have someone to coach us and hold the space for us as we light up, find our voice and speak it out to the world. Fear is the biggest internal obstacle to achieving anything and the best way to overcome it is through action. Lead, inspire, be the charismatic wayfinder and mark out the way for others to follow. I've done it by daring to start a business and believe I have something of value to offer. What's your vision? Whatever it is, begin it. If you are a writer, be a writer. If you are a leader, be a leader. If you are a scientist, astronaut, communicator, homemaker or a long-distance runner, begin. Take the first step into being.

A Summary To Stir That Female Giant Within…

- Balance your mind and access your own intuitive guidance system
- Pay attention to your dreams, take cues from nature
- Unlock your creativity
- Get a new window on your world – a 360 degree view and ask: what have I not seen?
- Breathe, move, play. Discover yourself and be life curious
- You are not your story
- Every day is 24 hours of possibility
- Follow your heart
- Reconnect your life to one of balance, purpose and joy
- See the beautiful mess inside each and every one of us
- Connect with the big outdoors
- Find people you love and what you are for
- Walk the change
- Get more for your life from less

And lastly... drink plenty of water!

It is time to step up and take our place. Embrace the rapture, do the work and accept the hero's quest. The world is waiting and the future may well just be the 3 Ws – The Web, The Weather and Women!! Be a part of it.

From Baby To Giant.
The Next Steps – And Beyond!

Don'ts and Dos

- × Don't put this book on the shelf and forget to do anything about it
- × Don't make the mistake of thinking 'It has always been this way so it will always be this way'. It doesn't have to.
- × Don't listen to the negative voices, tell them to 'go fetch'.
- × Don't play small, or nice or sorry. It serves no one.
- × Don't think you made the biggest mistake of your life. You haven't. Make it your best learning and be like cheese. Improve with age.
- ✓ **Do start with what you have and then seek those you love. Surround yourself with them.**
- ✓ **Do supercharge your life by finding the balance.**
- ✓ **Do tell an inspiring and appreciative story about yourself and your life.**
- ✓ **Do find your purpose and take it to the world.**

If you are inspired to take action and would like to work with Life Reconnected visit the website or email info@lifereconnected.co.uk
We look forward to meeting you.

About The Author

Penny C McClean, BSSc Hons Psychology, is a personal development trainer with a long career in supporting women through group work. She has worked for over 20 years in the community and voluntary sector in Northern Ireland and recently trained in London as an NLP Practitioner and professional coach. Penny began her own business after a period of huge personal change and as a way to answer what she sees as the need for women to become inspired in their lives again. She is also a new media author and speaker, interested in motivational change for women and is also a trained Walking Group Leader.

Penny resides in Northern Ireland but is constantly inspired by and works with women from all over Ireland, the UK and the rest of the English-speaking world.

About Life Reconnected

Life Reconnected is a business that provides training, coaching and capacity building for women. It provides coaching programmes for individual change in a group setting, individual coaching packages and group Team Building/Life Reconnecting days. *Life Reconnected* also develops resources for trainers in all fields of training who are keen to develop their style that is inclusive and empowering to women.

The key feature of a *Life Reconnected* programme is creative problem solving using NLP, co-active coaching, walking and connecting with the big outdoors and nature to bring about purposeful individual change. It uses models of psychology and ways of engaging that are mindful of the particular needs of women in managing change in their lives and that empowers them to become leaders in those lives and in turn inspire our young women leaders of the future.

Visit www.lifereconnected.co.uk

or email info@lifereconnected.co.uk for further information.

Author Acknowledgements

Best measured in connections and love my journey has been far. To my fellow Big Stretchers who kick started this sorry ass back to a life reconnected and to my friends, you know who you are, I give huge thanks.

To the women who read and took the time to give me their expertise and constructive criticism on a draft of this book (Lesley, Helen, Joan, Liz, Linda and her sister Helen and Rosie and Ailie), I am immensely appreciative.

For the scores of other women I have had the pleasure of sharing the talking conversations about women and change over the last number of years from London to Spain, New York to the Channel Islands I give more thanks and say you inspire me immensely.

To Norma who gave me the HALT, pointed out the green field and told me to get up off my knees.

To the hundreds of personal bloggers who inspire me daily and to a few I have to give a particular shout out to:

Kathy at Reinventing the Event Horizon:
(www.reinventingtheeventhorizon.wordpress.com)

Deborah at The Monster In Your Closet:
(www.deborah-bryan.com)

Pat at Back On My Own:
(www.backonmyown.wordpress.com)

Jo at Jo Bryant:
(www.jobryantnz.wordpress.com)

Lou at Pissy Kitty's Litter Box:
(www.pissykittyslitterbox.com)

To my coach Jessica who held the space, asked the questions and found the places my demon and I were hiding, thank you.

Recommended Reading

I could list a thousand books, websites, blogs and other resources to help inspire you as they did me but to keep the list short I'm including all that I have referred to or taken instruction from in my text.

Beck, Martha *Finding Your Way in A Wild New World*, Piatkus, 2012

Brampton, Sally *Shoot the Damn Dog, A Memoir Of Depression*, Bloomsbury, 2008

Burton, Kate *Coaching With NLP For Dummies*, Wiley 2011

Dickson, Anne *A Woman In Your Own Right*, Quartet Books, 1982

Lynch, Margaret M. Transformational Coach www.margaretmlynch.com

Simmons, Annette *Whoever Tells The Best Story Wins:The Subjective Side Of Business* in *Business The Ultimate Resource*, A&C Black, 2006

Steinhouse, Robbie *How To Coach With NLP,* Prentice Hall Business, 2010

Lightning Source UK Ltd.
Milton Keynes UK
UKOW03f1812210813

215767UK00016B/843/P